THE BLEEDING SKY

My Mother's Journey Through the Fire

As told to:

Louis Brandsdorfer

The Bleeding Sky

June 17,1987

I write this on the day of the funeral of my stepfather Maylech Spiegel. He was 85 years old when he died. He married my mother 14 years ago, a few years after my father died. Maylech, like my parents, was a survivor and his death was another reminder of how time was running out for the witnesses of the Holocaust.

I grew up in Brooklyn, New York. The community I lived in was populated with Holocaust survivors. Whenever they got together they would talk about the war. There seemed a need for many of the survivors to tell their stories, but the uniqueness of their experience did not dawn on me until I grew up and left New York. Outside of the city I found a very limited knowledge of the Holocaust.

In 1970 my father died. With him died the details of his personal experience in the war. As much as he told me I could not reconstruct in detail his story. I decided not to let my mother's story be lost too.

Over a period of time, I sat with my mother, recorded her stories of the war and organized this book. I also read everything I could find on the war and the Holocaust. I also found other children of survivors doing the same things, and for the same reasons.

My family, like the families of other survivors, was small. But it had once been large. Had it not been for the war I might have known 2 sets of grandparents, over a dozen sets of aunts and uncles, and countless cousins. Of my mother's family only she and one sister survived the war. On my father's side only my father and 2 of his brothers.

In getting my mother to talk about the war I asked her a lot of questions about her childhood and about her family. The more she talked about her home the more she remembered about her parents, brothers and sisters. And in her talking about them I felt I got to know them at least for a little while.

So this book took on a second purpose. It became a way of remembering those that did not survive, a way of keeping their memories alive. It was what the victims wanted. It was the same thing the survivors themselves wanted. It was one of the reason they told their stories so often.

Elie Wiesel said in explaining his passion to remember the Holocaust, "I feel that, having survived, I owe something to the dead. That was their obsession, to be remembered. Anyone who does not remember betrays them again."

I was also taken with a quote from Joseph Gottfarstein's book, "Judaism" that I found in Azriel Eisenberg's book, "Witness to the Holocaust." The quote was from the last Musar talk Rabbi Nahum Yanchiker, the Headmaster of the Slabodka Musar-Yeshiva near Kovno Lithuania, gave his students. Musar means an exercise in moral discipline.

As the Rabbi spoke the door of the Yeshiva was opened and someone yelled, "The Germans are coming."

The Rabbi stood up and told his students to flee and save themselves. He warned them about the dangers ahead and told them to always remember their people and their Yeshiva.

His last words to his students were these, "And do as our holy Sages had done-pour forth your words and cast them into letters. This will be the greatest retribution that you can wreak upon these wicked ones. Despite the raging wrath of our foes the holy souls of your brothers and sisters will remain alive. These evil ones schemed to blot out their names from the face of the earth; but a man cannot destroy letters. For words have wings; they mount up to the heavenly heights and they endure for eternity."

Louis Brandsdorfer

About the cover:

The top cover photo is of the Zionist youth organization of Boleslawiec, Poland. It was taken in 1937 along the river Prosna. The ruins of King Boleslaw's castle are in the background. Mala Liss, my mother, is standing in the center wearing a dark skirt and light sweater. The rest of the photo and who is pictured is on pages 190 and 191. The bottom photo is the train tracks and entrance to Birkenau, Auschwitz.

Maps and Photos:

Copies of my mother's audio recordings, plus additional information and links, can be found at ***thebleedingsky.com*** The recordings are in Yiddish.

The Bleeding Sky

And it shall come to pass, that in all the land, saith the lord, two parts therein shall be cut off and die; but the third part shall be left therein.

And I will bring the third part through the fire, and will refine them as silver is refined, and will try them as gold is tried: I will say, it is my people: and they shall say, the Lord is my God.

Zechariah 13:8,9

The Bleeding Sky

1

There is so much to tell of my experiences in the Second World War. Where do I start?

I recently had a telephone conversation with a friend from concentration camp. Her name is Shindala. During the war her last name was Lacher. Today it is Springer. She called me and said, "Mala, I was just thinking about the time you saved my life."

I laughed and said, "You know I was recently thinking about the time you saved mine."

I didn't remember doing anything that could have saved Shindala's life so I asked her to tell me about it.

She reminded me of the time we were working at the 103rd kommando in Birkenau, Auschwitz. The 103rd kommando was called an Ausser Kommando, which meant an outside command. She needed a couple of cigarettes to bribe a certain Kapo. Kapo meant foreman or overseer. This Kapo was in charge of the laundry, and for a couple of cigarettes the Kapo would give her a job in the laundry.

In the laundry the work was easier. It was warm and they got a little more soup than we did on the 103rd kommando. At the time I was dealing on the camp's black market and my dealings were going very well. She asked me to lend her some cigarettes. I told her I would lend her all that I could.

The cigarettes I lent her, I remember, were German cigarettes called Yosma. With them she bribed the Kapo and got a job in the laundry. Later she paid me back the cigarettes. She felt that getting that job actually saved her life.

Then she asked me to tell her how it was that she saved my life.

So I reminded her of an incident that happened during the march from Auschwitz. In January 1945, when the Russians were nearing Auschwitz, the Germans evacuated us with the rest of the camp. For days we were force marched through deep snow. At times the snow was up to our knees. On my shoulders I carried a blanket and some bread. I got very tired and was feeling sick. Both sides of the road were lined with people the Germans had shot when they could not walk any more.

I got very angry thinking about those poor people. They had suffered and survived so much. For them to die now when the war's end seemed so near seemed so tragic to me. I was so tired I just wanted to lie down and let the Germans shoot me too.

Shindala saw that I was about to give up. She took me under one arm and Reginka Storch, a friend from Warsaw, took hold of my other arm. Shindala said to me, "Mala, listen. Hear the guns? In the distance you can see the fires from the front. Those are Russian guns. In any minute the Germans will run away and leave us here. Come get yourself together."

She took the bundle from my shoulders and threw it away. "We have suffered so much," she said and started pointing to the people who had been shot and were now lying by the side of the road, "And now you want to give up and end up like these others?"

Shindala and Reginka started to drag me along. After about 10 minutes I started to cry and started walking, and about 2 hours later the Germans led us into a barn and let us rest.

The next day they loaded us into wagons for the rest of the journey. If it hadn't been for Shildala I would have been shot and left to die by the side of the road.

I mentioned dealing on the black market in Auschwitz. It's very interesting how it worked and how I got involved in it.

Dealing, trading, or in Yiddish, "haundling", was a way of life for my family. It was the way my husband earned his living. It was the way many Jews, especially in Eastern Europe, lived. Many professions and guilds were closed to Jews. So they became dealers and traders.

In the camps, and even in the Warsaw ghetto, I knew that I would have to deal to survive. The amount of food we received was just enough to let us starve slowly to death. Without extra food I would have died. All the people who lived through the concentration camps had to deal in some way to survive. We called it, "black marketing", and since it was against the law it was a way to fight the Germans. For most of us it was the only way.

Dealing in the traditional sense meant trading at a profit. In Auschwitz it meant that and more. It meant trading goods or services to improve your situation and your chances of survival.

Many years after the war I met a lady who had also survived Auschwitz. She was there as a political prisoner. The Germans did not know that she was Jewish. The conditions in the camp for her were horrible, but she knew that for the other Jews they were even worse.

Non-Jews did not have to go through the selections. Selections were inspections that were periodically conducted to see if one was still fit to work and to continue living. Violations of the rules brought non-Jews severe punishment.

For Jews those same violations brought death. Non-Jews were allowed to receive packages from home, and many also received Red Cross packages. Those packages were the main source of supplementary food in the camp. Jews were not allowed to receive any Red Cross packages, and of course by the time I was in Auschwitz we did not have anyone at home to send us anything.

When she heard how long I had survived in Auschwitz, she asked, "How did you survive? How did you live through that hell? For a Jew to survive Auschwitz was a miracle."

I told her, "Haundling, that's how I survived."

Even in relatively good times Jews looked to deal to improve their lot. I remember a story my father told me. When he was a young man, living in Wielun, he was called up to serve in the Russian army. This was in 1903 and at that time Poland was not an independent country. The Wielun region, like the rest of Poland was part of Russia. Poles and the Jews of Poland felt no loyalty towards Russia. Russia was seen as a foreign occupier. But five years of military service was mandatory for all young men with severe punishment dealt out to anyone caught trying to avoid their military service.

The post my father was stationed to was in central Siberia. When he got there he was asked if he had any skills. He said he was a tailor because he was learning that trade before he was called up. At the post there were five tailors. The head tailor's five years of service were almost up, and one of the other tailors was to be assigned his position. Since the post was soon to be short a tailor my father was assigned to that group.

During my father's training he learned that the head tailor was selling cloth in the nearby villages. The head tailor would order enough material to make a certain number of uniforms. He would order enough to make them all a large size. When they were actually made they were all of different sizes. Since the head tailor also kept the records, the difference did not show up. The material was of heavy wool and of very good quality. In Siberia that cloth was valuable. In fact the head tailor was getting rich from that extra cloth.

My father realized that the position of head tailor would not become vacant again for a long time. He decided that, if he wanted to become the head tailor, now was the time to go after it. My father knew that he would have to do something in order to get appointed to that position since he was really the least experienced of all the tailors there. He decided that the only way to do it was to befriend the camp commandant. The commandant would be the one appointing the new head tailor.

On my father's next day off he went into town and bought the most expensive set of wine goblets he could find. He had them engraved with the commandant's name. When he returned to the post he went and stood outside the commandant's house.

That evening the commandant and his wife returned home and saw my father standing outside holding a package under his arm. The commandant asked him what he wanted. My father told him that he had written home and told his family how good a commanding officer he had. His family sent this package as a gift to the commandant. He told him that the gift was from Warsaw. Items from Warsaw were considered of high quality all over Russia. When the commandant's wife heard that the gift was from Warsaw she ask to see it.

My father was shown into the house. He unwrapped the goblets and set them on the table. The wife's eyes widened when she saw the goblets. The commandant said to my father, "They are beautiful, but I cannot accept them. It is against the law for me to accept a gift from a man under my command."

The commandant's wife took her husband aside and whispered in his ear. When he returned he asked my father how much he wanted for the goblets. My father said he did not want anything for them. He said that his family was rich, which wasn't true, and that the gift was from them. It wasn't his to sell. Since the commandant's name was inscribed on the goblets there was nothing else he could do with them. He begged the commandant to take the goblets. When he begged he made sure the commandant's wife heard him.

Finally the commandant relented and accepted the goblets. He told my father to thank his family and asked him not to tell anyone about this since he did not want to encourage that sort of thing. As my father was leaving the commandant told him if he needed anything to feel free to ask him.

A month went by. It was getting near the time for the head tailor to leave. My father went to the commandant and told him that he would like the appointment as head tailor. The commandant told him he was concerned that my father did not have enough experience. My father assured him that he could do the job. The commandant told him he would see what he could do, but made him no promises.

The day the head tailor left, the other tailors lined up to be addressed by the commandant. As he addressed them he announced that my father was to be the new head tailor. Everyone except my father was surprised.

The rest of his time in the army my father had a thriving business in pieces of cloth. His position as head tailor also allowed him to remain at the post during the Russian Japanese war. The war started in 1904, less then a year after his appointment. All the other tailors were transferred to the infantry and sent east to the war.

My father's best friend in the army was another Orthodox Jew. His name was Aaron. After the army the two of them returned to Wielun and Aaron married my father's oldest sister. My father had enough money saved to buy a couple of sewing machines and to go into business. The lesson my father said was, "Anyone can be bribed, even a king. All you have to know is his price and how to approach him."

In every camp I came into I checked on how I could get into dealing. I came to Auschwitz in July 1943 from Majdanek.

When I came to Auschwitz I had nothing of value on me. The way to start dealing was to save a piece of bread from one's food. The whole summer I tried to save one piece of bread. But I could not save any. Each day we had to get up at 3:00 A.M. It was still the middle of the night. We were chased out of our barracks. By 4:00 we were lined up on the Appel. Appel meant roll call or head count, but we called the space in front of our barracks where the head count was held the Appel. We were given some tea and marched to work. At noon we got some watered down soup. In the evening we marched back to the camp. We were lined up and kept waiting on the Appel till the SS counted us. This roll call took up to two hours. Then we got a piece of foul bread. Once a week we got a half-inch thick slice of sausage. I was so hungry by then that I could not give up that piece of bread or that sausage.

I needed that piece of bread so I could start dealing. I knew that only by dealing would I survive. But I was afraid that if I didn't eat that piece of bread I would not live to the next day. The whole summer of 1943 in Auschwitz, I tried to figure out a way to get an extra piece of bread.

A piece of bread could be traded in the camp for an onion or an apple. In the hospital, called the Rewier, an onion or an apple could be traded among the sick for 2 or 3 pieces of bread. That's how I hoped to get started dealing. But I could not get that one piece of bread.

In September, between the High Holy days of Rosh Hasanah and Yom Kippur, a great piece of luck happened to me. One of the greatest pieces of luck in the whole world. While I was dreaming of just one piece of bread I got 46 loaves of bread.

Tradition says that each person is judged in heaven, between the High Holy days, whether to live or die in the coming year. This must have been my judgment in heaven.

That whole summer the work group I was in was dressed in uniforms taken from Russian prisoners of war. There were 500 women in that group. In September we were ordered to exchange the uniforms for women's clothing. We were brought a pile of clothes to change into.

I was handed a blouse and skirt. They were both navy blue in color. As I was seeing if it fit I felt something fat in the lining of the skirt. I pulled apart the seam and pulled out 20 American dollars.

Standing next to me was one of my friends. Her maiden name was Salla Butter. Today her name is Salla Hyman and she lives in Brooklyn. She grabbed me and started kissing me and said, "Mala, that $20 is worth 20 loaves of bread."

In the skirt there was even more money. I pulled out another $26. It created a lot of excitement among us. We took $10, Salla knew where we could go and start dealing.

The 103rd kommando's job was to build the roads in and around the camp.

We were 500 women in that kommando. We were split into groups of 50. One group split rocks. One group cleared the stones from the field. One group loaded lorries and pushed them along tracks. One group set the paving stones. This way we worked as a team in the fields. 2000 men worked there too. They built the buildings that were used as barracks and a hospital for the SS.

Among the 2000 men that were working on the barracks were Volksdeutsch. Volksdeutsch were Poles of German descent. They were the machine operators. They told us to smuggle out of the camp dollars or gold. Sometimes they would ask for other things. Once they asked for silk kerchiefs. They paid us mostly with cigarettes, and sometimes with food, like eggs and butter, but those were hard to smuggle back into the camp. The easiest things to bring back into camp were cigarettes. Cigarettes in the camp were the most expensive things. They were just like money.

Four cigarettes were equal to a dollar, or a small bread. The non-Jewish women received packages from home. Those that smoked would trade things from those packages for cigarettes. So when we came back into the camp with cigarettes we were able to buy almost anything we wanted.

That's how my haundling worked in Auschwitz.

For most of the time I was in Auschwitz I was in the 103rd kommando. We helped build a whole city for the SS on the fields of Birkenau. When we finished the buildings in the summer of 1944, the Germans brought their wounded from the eastern front. It cost us a lot of blood to build that city. Every day 30 to 35 of the women among us died or got sick. And every day the SS replaced them with new ones so there would still be 500 in the kommando. Still when we were finished I was glad to see the Allied airplanes come and destroy the buildings.

In 1944 we heard that the war was going badly for Germany. But it was only rumors; we didn't know what was really happening. But when I saw the planes bomb the buildings I had a feeling I just might survive the war after all.

Once when a group of us were watching the planes bomb outside the camp a German matron saw me jump up and laugh. In my excitement I wasn't careful to look if anyone was watching us. She came over and hit me hard across the head. As she pointed to the crematorium she said, "You dummy, the chimney is the only way you'll leave this camp. You won't live to see the end of the war."

But even she could not stop my happiness, for I felt in my heart that I would survive.

2
BEGINNINGS

I started to tell my story from the middle. Now I'll go back to the beginning, before the war started.

My parents were born in Poland. Poland was part of Russia at the time. My father, Mordechai Liss, was born in 1880 in the city of Wielun. My mother's name was Blima. Her maiden name was Schenk. She was born in 1882 in a small village near the town of Boleslawiec called Wojcin. Boleslawiec was about 30 kilometers from Wielun.

In 1906 they married and seven children followed; first was my brother Gavriel, born in September 1909. I was the second, born January 1912, then came my sister Eudal in December 1913, next my brother Wolf, born October 1915, my sisters Fay in May 1917, Yenta in March 1919, and Sara on the Saturday between Rosh Hashanah and Yom Kippur in September 1923. Between my last two sisters my mother had a stillbirth.

The size of our family, at that time, wasn't considered large. The apartment we lived in wasn't large either. It was on the ground floor of a two-story building owned by a Polish farmer. The house was on one of the town's main streets. We lived in the front half of the ground floor, and the farmer's family lived in the back. Upstairs lived a single man who worked in the local school. In the back yard the farmer kept some of his farm animals.

Our apartment had three rooms. They were very large rooms. Two we used to live in and one, the front one, was for my father's business. At night some sewing machines were moved aside, and a bed was put out for my two brothers.

My father's business was cap making. He had a combination workshop and store. Some of his merchandise was also sold to other stores in other towns. A lot of the caps were made to order as part of uniforms for fraternal organizations, the military, police and firemen.

As the other children grew up they went into the business to help my father. As the oldest daughter my job was in the house, mostly to care for my younger brother and sisters as my mother went to run the store part of the business. My father also employed some salesmen to help sell the caps in other towns.

Life was slow and comfortable in a small town. Boleslawiec had about two-dozen paved streets. At the edge of town was a river called the Prosna. The Prosna flowed into the Warta, and the Warta into the Oder. In the summer the whole town went swimming in the Prosna.

At various times in the town's history, like the rest of Poland, it had been controlled at different times by each of the neighboring countries. In medieval times it had been the capitol of a Polish kingdom. Outside of town there still stood the ruins of the king's castle. The town took its name from the king who built that castle. But in 1939 it was just a small town on the western edge of Poland just a kilometer from the German border.

I remember growing up in Boleslawiec very happy. The town had about 500 families, with about 2500 people. Jews made up about a quarter of the population. There weren't many of the problems between the Jews and the Christians that there were in the larger cities. We lived and traded together in peace.

There were some Poles in our town who were openly anti-Semitic, but very few. One of the better-known ones was the brother of the farmer in whose house we lived.

The farmer's family and ours were close. Their name was Chmielewski. Mrs. Chmielewski treated me and my brothers and sisters as her own.

Mr. Chmielewski, whose first name was Ignash, had a brother named Antoush. They built their houses next to each other, separated by a large yard. The yard was closed off from the street by a gate.

Antoush Chmielewski was a Polish patriot and an anti-Semite. In our town, among the Poles, he was only remembered for his patriotism. I don't remember him much, since he died when I was young. I only remember stories about him.

On the other side of Antoush Chmielewski house, away from his brother's, was the house of the town's rabbi. The rabbi's house was also the yeshiva or Hebrew school. On the wall of Antoush's house, facing the rabbi's, he constructed a large cross, which he painted red. It couldn't be seen from the street, only from the rabbi's house.

The rabbi told how one morning he greeted Antoush. The rabbi said, "Good morning, neighbor."

Antoush answered, "We shall not be neighbors long. Either you will soon move away, or I will. But I will not allow this situation to go on much longer."

And soon after that Antoush died.

I was six years old, in 1918, when the world war ended and the new Polish state was being created. To the west of our town was a forest that on one side bordered the town and on the other side bordered Germany. Antoush Chmielewski and some other men went to the game warden of the forest and demanded some documents concerning the forest. They wanted to make sure the forest became part of the new Poland. The warden refused and shots were fired. I was standing out in front of the house when the wagon with Antoush's body was brought back to town. The man driving the wagon told me to run inside and open the gate to the yard. I did and watched as they brought his body inside. There was a lot of crying and wailing in the two Chmielewski households.

Two weeks before Passover, in 1937, I married Alter Goldrat. At first my father was against our getting married. He said that Alter was poor, but we persisted and he gave in. Alter was my first cousin. Our mothers were sisters. It was a small wedding, just for the family. We moved into an apartment across the street from my parents.

My husband's real name was Ben-Zion. As a child he was sickly, and his mother followed an old superstition of renaming him Alter, which meant old. It was believed that by renaming a sick child one could fool the angel of death into thinking that he was mistaken. When he came for a child, and learned that he was called Alter, he would think that this could not be the one he was looking for and would leave the child alone. So they called him Alter. The name stayed with him even after he grew up.

On June 16, 1938 we had a child, a daughter. Her Jewish name was Esther Figala. In Polish she was called Falunya. When she first started talking she could not say Falunya. Instead she would say Nunya. So we called her Nunyala. She was a beautiful child.

When my brother Gavriel served in the Polish army he was stationed in Posnan. He liked the city very much, and after his time in the army was over he moved there. A man who had once worked for my father had moved there earlier, and Gavriel had remained good friends with him. My brother went to work for his friend after he moved to Posnan.

Gavriel married a first cousin of ours from Wielun. Her name was Hinda Ruthy Liss. We called her Ruschka. They got married in Wielun in October 1937, about six months after I got married, and they settled in Posnan. They had one daughter named Pearl. My other brother and sisters were still single when the war began.

Alter's business was dealing in live poultry, buying them locally and selling them in the city. He had learned the business from his father. Two or three days before the outbreak of the war Alter returned from Lodz. He said to me, "You can see preparations for war in Lodz. Pack up your things. You're leaving the border area."

First he wanted just our daughter and me to go, but I insisted that we would not leave unless he came too.

Alter's brother Leipush had a small truck. He was in partnership with a few others in a trucking company. Alter made quick arrangements with Leipush to move some of our possessions. Alter, Leipush, Nunyala and myself squeezed into the front seat.

We soon found the main roads impassable. They were clogged with people and their animals leaving the border area just like us. We traveled the smaller roads. Lodz was only 130 kilometers or about 80 miles, but still we could not get there on Wednesday. Near the end of the day we stopped at the house of a relative and spent the night.

Thursday morning we started out again and the roads were even worse. Traveling was very slow even on the side roads. There was no road that wasn't full of people heading for Lodz. It took us all day but finally by sundown we reached the city. Friday morning the war started.

We stayed at Piotrkowska 85 with a cousin of mine named Seasel Sthiller. Piotrkowska was a main street that ran through the middle of the city. Seasel had a 3-room apartment for her, her husband and their child. But Seasel's mother and 3 sisters and the 3 of us stayed there too. By Friday evening we heard how badly the war was going. The next day Alter's brother, Leipush, came over and told us of what he had seen.

After he left us at my cousin's a group of Polish officers forced him to drive them to the Romanian border. From there they escaped to England. The officers offered to take Leipush along, but he said, "No." He had to return home to his wife and children.

The next day, or maybe even that day, the Germans started bombing Lodz. We all went and stayed in the cellar.

Every day we heard that the Germans were getting closer to Lodz. People started leaving the city any way they could. The women decided that the men should run away. We were sure that the Germans wouldn't do anything to the women and children, but the men might have been in danger. My husband and the other men from the building fled the city. I stayed there with my daughter.

Lodz had a large German population so the city was not badly damaged by the Germans. In a house across the street from my cousin's apartment lived a German family. The day the war started the house looked dark and deserted. But a few days later, when the Germans entered the city, all the lights were on and the house had a very festive air about it.

The Germans entered Lodz and continued their advance into Poland. A few days later my mother and my sisters Yenta and Sara came to my cousin's house in Lodz. Their feet were all blistered from walking.

They had left home the day after I did to take some of the family's valuables to a relative in a nearby village for safekeeping. They spent the night there. Early in the morning they set out for home but were caught on the road when the war started.

My mother told us of their running from the Germans. With my mother and sisters was my younger brother Wolf. About 50 kilometers from home they crossed the river Warta. There the Polish army was going to make a stand. A group of young men got together to join. My brother Wolf was among them. He said he wanted to fight the Germans. My mother pleaded with him not to go but to no avail. My mother and sisters kissed him good-bye and continued running.

The German advance was so fast that by the next day they learned that the Germans were already in the town in front of them. There was no place for them to run to so they turned around and headed for Lodz.

The next day, after my mother came to Lodz, my daughter and I, together with my mother and two sisters, returned home to our town. We left because my cousin's apartment was too crowded, and we had heard nothing from home and were very worried. We felt we had to return home and find out what had happened.

My cousin arranged for one of her neighbors to drive us home, but on the outskirts of the city a group of German soldiers confiscated the car. The neighbor returned to his home, and we started walking to ours.

We walked all day. That night we spent by the side of the road. I remember the weather during those first days and nights of the war as being very beautiful. In the morning we set out again. The day was the first day of Rosh Hashanah, the

Jewish New Year. By midday, Mr. Chmielewski and his wife, the farmers in whose house we lived, drove by in their horse drawn wagon. They had also spent the last few days in Lodz and were heading home to see what had happened. We rode home the rest of the way with them.

The whole way home Mr. Chmielewski complained about the great horse he had lost. As they were leaving Lodz, Mr. Chmielewski caught a cavalry horse that had been riderless. A short while later, a group of Germans soldiers confiscated the horse, but he carried on as if he had lost his life's savings.

As we neared the house my father approached. I almost didn't recognize him. The Germans had cut off his beard, and in the two weeks I hadn't seen him, he had gotten very old.

He told us of the troubles he had had. By 7:00 in the morning, the day the war broke out, the Germans were already in our town. They forced everyone out of their houses and chased them across the fields into Germany. They threw a hand grenade into almost every house and burned down about half the town.

The Germans kept the townspeople in a field. The Jews were separated out from the other townspeople. The German soldiers stole any valuables the Jews had on them and treated them very harshly. A leading Jew of the town, named Shimsa Russek, was singled out for the harshest treatment. Some of the Poles from our town pointed him out as a rich Jew. He returned home barely alive.

About 8 to 10 days later, after the Germans were already deep into Poland, they let some of the townspeople return home. First they let the women and children go, and a few days later they let the men go too. First the Poles, a little later the Jews. The first to return to our home was my sister Fay and then my father.

In a way we were the lucky ones. The Germans had not burned my apartment or my father's. The house of his Polish neighbor was burned, and he just took over my father's apartment, while my father was being held by the Germans. My father could do nothing about it. So he and my mother and sisters moved in with me.

My apartment was 2 rooms on the second floor. My father brought over 3 sewing machines and a lot of material. In the apartment where I once lived with my husband and daughter now lived 4 or 5 families. One of my neighbors, a man never considered very smart, also came to live with us. Once I overheard him say that he wished my husband would not come home. He feared that my husband would not let him stay there, and he had nowhere else to go. That's what the war started doing to people, making them wish for another to die so that they wouldn't have to suffer.

The Germans caught Alter on the road. For a week they held him in prison and then he was released. He returned home 10 days after I did. When he walked into the house there was a lot of hugging and kissing. He looked very bad. He said he prayed day and night that he would see our daughter and me one more time.

As the Polish army retreated in front of the German advance my brother's unit was pulled back to help defend Warsaw. During the defense of the capital, in the town of Otwock, my brother was wounded in the head by shrapnel. He remained in a hospital in Otwock for a few weeks until he recovered. At home we had received no news from him the whole time and feared him dead.

When he was released he went to Lodz. He wanted to find a friend of his and talk him into going to Russia with him, but instead Wolf was talked into going home by some of his relatives. Everyone told him how his mother cried when she thought him dead.

He came home thinking it would only be for a short while, but he never did make it to Russia. As the time passed it became harder and harder for him to leave. My parents came to depend on him so much. Maybe if he had gone to Russia, instead of coming home, he would have survived the war. But at that time who could have imagined what the future held for us.

The beginning of the war was during the High Holy Days. Our synagogue was burned down when the Germans first came into the town. The Jews got together in someone's house to pray, but when the Germans found out they came and dragged the men outside, beat them, and warned them that Jews would be shot if they tried to assemble again.

Almost every day after that, new rules were issued for Jews. Jews were not allowed to walk on the sidewalk. Stores were posted with signs saying Jews not allowed. All Jews had to wear a yellow Jewish star on their coat whenever they were out in public. All Jews, no matter what age, had to register with a Jewish authority called the Judenrat. This way, whenever the Germans needed to assemble Jews for work, they went to the Judenrat and ordered as many as they needed. The Judenrat had to provide them or the town's Jews would suffer even more.

The Judenrat's responsibilities also included the Jewish community's health, welfare needs, food rationing, and housing. Hershel Scurka, one of the leading Jews of our town, was appointed to head the Judenrat. Under him was a man named Moshe Maier Prince. Moshe Maier was a leading Zionist from our district.

The first thing the Judenrat was instructed to do was to collect all the gold, silver and furs that the Jews had. Needless to say they collected very little. It all went into hiding or was given to friendly Christians for safekeeping.

One of the jobs they had the Jews do was remove the large wooden crosses from the streets and roads. All over Poland the Church had put up wooden crosses along the roads. They were heavy crosses. I remember when one had fallen and crushed a young man's foot. His name was Hetush Kohen, and they had to remove his foot.

Also the Jews were assigned to care for the grounds around the main buildings in the town. I remember my sisters going to cut the grass on the market square. The grass grew between the paving stones in the square. My sisters were given spoons to dig out the grass.

Every day it seemed to get worse and worse. Just when we thought it might end a new rule would come out and make life even harder. And the rules also made life dangerous. It seemed that all violations of the rules were punishable by death. I remember a woman named Leah Froman. She went crazy after watching the Germans execute her son. He was killed for violating one of their rules.

I remember going out for a walk with my husband and daughter on a Friday evening. As we walked a man approached us and slapped my husband in the face. We stood there not knowing what had happened until the man said, "You dumb Jew. Don't you know that you have to salute me?"

My husband said that he didn't know who he was. The man opened his coat and revealed an SS button on the lapel of his jacket.

After that we were too afraid to go out walking again. My daughter was so frightened by the incident that every time she saw someone in uniform walking down the street she would run home hysterically and yell, "Daddy, hide, a German is coming."

Every day there was more to fear. Normal ways to earn a living were being denied to Jews. There was rationing of food for everyone, but for Jews the rationing was more severe. Everyone looked for a way to earn a living under these conditions. Our family, in partnership with some other families, started to smuggle soap from Lodz and sell it on the black market. Later, when the Jews of Lodz were put into a closed ghetto, we started to make the soap ourselves.

A neighbor in our apartment building, named Pinkus Holse, would sell the soap throughout the town. Once a Polish townsman was caught with the soap and informed the authorities from where he had bought it. Two Germans came to Pinkus Holse's apartment. One of the Germans we called the Shooter. He was called that because for no reason at all he would shoot people.

I remember the Shooter as being tall. I don't remember his face. I was too scared to look into the Germans' faces. Most of the time I was too afraid to go out of the apartment. When I had to, and I passed one of them, I always turned my face to the ground.

From our apartment we were able to hear the Germans beating and questioning Pinkus. We were very frightened because in the middle of our apartment we had a large box of soap. There was no place in the apartment to hide that large a box. After a time Pinkus told the Germans that he got the soap from a man named Itzhak Moshe Goldrat. Itzhak Moshe was one of Alter's brothers. Up until the day before he was also living in the apartment with us. He had just moved to another apartment building.

The Germans came to our apartment. I ran around trying to hide the soap, but there was no time or place to hide it all. My father stayed calm as he answered the door. I grabbed my daughter and held on to her as I shook like a leaf. The Germans were a very clean people. When my father opened the door they saw that the floor had just been cleaned and waxed so they didn't enter the apartment. They asked if his name was Goldrat. He said, "No," and showed them papers that his name was Liss. My father told them that Goldrat had moved out, and was now living with a family named Verva.

It was a miracle that we cleaned and waxed the floor that morning. Had the Germans come in they certainly would have seen the box of soap, and that would have cost us our lives. It was also a miracle that Itzhak Moshe had moved out of the apartment.

The Germans went to where my brother-in-law was living. We had gotten word to him about what was happening so he went into hiding. The Germans searched his apartment, found nothing, but left word that he was wanted for questioning at the police station.

We knew Itzhak Moshe would have to turn himself in. If he did not, and was caught, he would be killed outright. We put some money together and bribed one of the Polish officials. A few days later my brother-in-law went to the police station, but by then everything had been taken care of.

Something happened that I will never forget. In our town lived a Jew named Smeal Prince. He was a widower with 5 children. His wife had died just before the war. He had a large house and he rented part of it out to help him get some money. The woman he rented it to was a Christian, and the wife of a

Polish officer who had escaped to England with part of the Polish army.

The mayor of our town was a Pole appointed by the Germans. We called the mayor Motele. Motele was the name of a rowdy young man who used to live in our town.

One day the mayor, his secretary, and the head of the post office tried to get into the woman's apartment. She barricaded the door so they couldn't get in. They went into Smeal Prince's part of the house, pushed a dresser aside, and forced open a door that led into her apartment.

The next day the woman went to the Germans to file rape charges against the mayor and the other two men. As a witness she gave the name of Smeal Prince and his oldest son, Kupple. The next day the German we called the Shooter came to Smeal Prince's house, took him and his son to the outskirts of town, and shot them both. So with no more witnesses against the 3 men the case was dropped.

The Germans picked on religious Jews the most. Once, two German soldiers stopped Alter outside of town. They were stationed in our town as policemen. Both Germans knew Alter. It was Friday and he was carrying two chickens he had just purchased for the Sabbath. The Germans made Alter cut off the chicken's heads. They knew that by killing the chickens that way it would make them non-kosher. They told Alter to take home the chicken and warned him that he had better eat them. Instead Alter sold the two chickens to a neighbor and bought two others and had the kosher butcher kill them.

The next day, during our Sabbath meal, the two Germans came to our apartment. They demanded to see the chickens. We showed them the chickens we were eating and one of them said to the other, "They're eating them. See, they're eating them."

They both laughed as they left the apartment. Only when we were sure they could not hear us did we break into laughter ourselves.

Others who were caught with contraband weren't as lucky as we were. I remember a young man named Lefkowitz. He was in a work camp, and he wrote his parents asking them to send him some silk stockings to trade with. His parents did so, but the Germans inspected the package and found the stockings. The young man was hanged for it.

Another young man from our town, named Prince, was killed as he worked as a forced laborer in a field. He was picking vegetables and tried to hide a carrot for himself. He was spotted by a German guard and shot on the spot.

The news of the war was bad for us. Our only hope was in a German defeat somewhere, but at that time they were unbeatable and our troubles seemed endless.

Late in 1941 the Germans confiscated our apartment. It was one of the larger apartments in the building. Too large for Jews they said, so we were forced to take a smaller one in the same building. It was so small that at night most of us had to go to sleep in the attics of some of our neighbors' houses. There was just enough room for the older people to sleep there and to do some cooking. We would get together there only during the day and to have our meals.

Every few weeks the Germans would order the Judenrat to assemble a certain number of Jews in the market square to be sent to labor camp. At first it was mostly the young single men who were ordered assembled. Later the young woman and married men went too.

In 1940, and early 1941, the Germans started setting up ghettos for the Jews in the larger cities. Lodz was the first, followed by Warsaw. In the small towns like ours there were no ghettos. Instead the Judenrat had to supply a certain number of Jews, demanded periodically by the Germans, to be sent to a labor camp. By 1942 they were also assembling Jewish families for what they said was resettlement to the east. It didn't take long to learn that resettlement meant concentration camp.

In some cities and towns the first Jews assembled by the Judenrats were the poor, the rich and the influential being able to bribe someone into letting them stay, at least a little longer. But this did not happen in our town. The men who ran our Judenrat were very honorable. In fact among the first Jews to be sent to labor camp were the two sons of Mosha Maier Prince, the man who was the second in charge of the Judenrat. Also a young man named Kuple Miller was one of the first to go. His family was one of the town's wealthiest.

Since my father was a hat maker the Germans ordered him to continue making hats, but now he was working for them. Whenever an assembly was called, my father would go to the Germans and plead with them not to take my younger brother Wolf. Since he was getting older and his eyesight was getting worse he said he needed his son to help him. Each time he went to plead they would let my brother remain in the town.

This went on for about a year. One day, word got back to us about an elderly neighbor who had died in a labor camp. My brother got very mad at my father. He said for my father not to go to plead with the Germans on his behalf anymore. He was ashamed that he was still at home while others, older than him, were suffering and dying in the camps.

It wasn't long after that that another assembly was ordered. My brother was the first to go. Also my husband and two youngest sisters, Yenta and Sara, and a number of my cousins were also taken. That was on the 15th of May, 1942. First they were taken to Wielun, the district capitol, then the men went to a camp near Posnan. My sisters and the other women were sent to a camp called Inowroclaw, which was 100 kilometers from Posnan.

A week or two later, one of my cousins returned from the camp near Posnan. He and a group of 5 other young men had escaped. He said that Wolf was with another group of six men that were also going to escape, and that Wolf would be home soon. We even received a letter from my brother that he posted during his escape, but he never came home. After the war I learned that his group was caught by the Germans, and all of them were hung. By the time we got his letter he was already dead.

The same day they took away my brother they also took away my husband. Every time my father went to plead for my brother I also went to bribe the mayor so that Alter would not be taken.

Whenever an assembly of Jews was called for I would make Alter go into hiding and take something of value that I had to the mayor's office. Once I gave away a set of expensive drapes. Once a gold watch. I had a large collection of porcelain, that I had been collecting from before the war, and piece by piece I gave it away.

Once my husband complained that when the war ended we'd be paupers since I was giving everything away. But I didn't care I just didn't want him taken away.

On the day they took Alter away I was very sick. I had a temperature of 103. Alter took me to the doctor, and he left me there with our child. As he said good-bye, he told me he feared that if he didn't go they might take the whole family.

So it was better that he went by himself. Again I pleaded with him to hide, but he did not listen.

It was the last time I saw him.

The next day I arranged, with a Christian who did business with Alter, to deliver some money to a cousin of mine in Wielun. I wanted my cousin to use the money to rescue Alter. Two days went by, and I heard that his group was still being held in Wielun. I had heard nothing from my cousin so I decided to go to Wielun myself.

Wielun was 30 kilometers from my hometown. I joined a group of women going to Wielun to try to rescue their husbands or sons. In a small village on the road to Wielun we were caught by some Germans who recognized us as Jewish. It was against the law for a Jew to travel without a police permit, but all they did was send us back to our town. They warned us that if any of us were caught again we would be sent to concentration camp.

The next day I removed the star from my coat and set out for Wielun, by myself, but by a different route.

It was a five-hour walk to Wielun. I came into the city around noontime. I learned that less than an hour before I got there the group of Jews from my town was taken out of the city. I couldn't find out where they were taken so I went to my cousin's house. When I asked him what had happened to the money I sent, he went pale. He said he thought the money was from his sister. Her husband was also in the same group with Alter. He thought he was to rescue his sister's husband, which is what he did.

His sister was Seasel Sthiller, in whose apartment in Lodz I stayed at the start of the war. Seasel and her family had moved back to Boleslawiec to avoid having to move into the ghetto when it was being established in Lodz.

I returned home very upset and broken. There was nothing more I could do.

A month later I received a letter from Alter from labor camp. I wrote back telling him about the attempted rescue in Wielun. He wrote a very angry letter to my cousin accusing him of knowingly using the money to rescue his brother-in-law instead of him. I was told that after my cousin read the letter he burned it so no one else could see it.

Fate works in strange ways. Seasel's husband, rescued instead of my husband, came home. Three months later during the last roundups of Jews, he, Seasel, and their child were taken. The transports they were on took them straight to their deaths. Had Alter come home I never would have gone into hiding. Instead of the Sthillers, Alter, Nunyala and myself would have been on that transport.

3
HIDING

For the next three months I lived in our small apartment with my parents, two sisters, Eudel and Fay, and my daughter. My mother's brother, Uncle Moshe, also lived with us at this time.

My oldest brother, Gavriel, and his family had been living in Posnan when the war started. The Germans sent them and the other Jews of Posnan to the city of Ostrow Lubelski in the east. Ostrow Lubelski was in the district of Lublin near the Russian border. The Germans designated the Lublin district as the Jewish district. We were told that in time all Jews would have to settle there.

For a few months before the war started, Eudel was living in Posnan with Gavriel. There she studied making false teeth out of clay. She was always very good at molding things with her hands.

After the war started Eudel came home. Soon she was helping people hide small valuables, such as jewels and gold pieces by burying them in small figurines. She made them out of the same kind of clay she had used to make false teeth.

In the middle of August, the third week in the month of Av, the Germans called the final assembly. The call was for all the rest of the Jews in the town. No Jew was to remain behind. The day before a Christian acquaintance came from the city of Wielun and told me that they were assembling all the Jews from there. I knew that this was the last of the Jews from the entire area. These assemblies were to make the district free of Jews.

In one of Alter's letters from concentration camp he warned me that if there was an assembly I could not get out of I should go into hiding with our daughter. He said that I would be sent to work but that the Germans were killing the children.

Before I left town I tried to get my whole family to go into hiding with me. But my father would not believe that the Germans would kill us. He would say, "They had taken Gavriel and his family into a camp over a year ago, and they were still alive." But I couldn't be sure what the Germans would do, so I wasn't going to take a chance. Especially with the life of my daughter.

I gathered up my Nunyala and a change of clothes for the two of us. I also took all the money I had, about 700 marks. As I was about to run out of the house my mother called me back. "You're leaving so fast," she said. "Please take the time to properly say good-bye, because I feel this maybe the last time I shall ever see you."

With tears running down everyone's cheeks we kissed each other good-bye. As I ran into the street my father ran after me with a kerchief in his hand. He wrapped it around me and kissed me. That was the last I saw of my parents.

For a few years before she moved to Posnan, my sister Eudel had been living at my uncle Moshe's. He was my mother's only brother and didn't have any children. One day he said to my mother, "Blimcha," my mother's name was Blima, but she was called Blimcha, "You have 5 daughters. Why doesn't one of them live with me?"

My sister Eudel heard my uncle, and said that she wanted to go. Since my uncle only lived a few houses away my mother said, "Yes." It hardly seemed like she was gone. She would eat and sleep at my uncle's, but ten times a day she would come home.

During the time my sister lived at my uncle's she also worked at his store. My uncle would buy grain from the farmers from the nearby villages and sell it in the town. My sister would work the scales when the farmers brought the grain. One of the farmers who dealt with my uncle was a Christian named Pannek. He was a very nice man, and he liked my sister because of how honest she was. He always insisted that she work the scales when he did business with my uncle. After the war began he said to her that if she or her family ever had to hide from the Germans they should come to him, and he'd hide them at his farm.

Pannek's farm was about one kilometer from our town. My daughter and I went there to hide. Pannek let us in and made a place for us in the attic of the stall. The stall was across the yard from his house. Pannek was in his fifties. Living with him were his wife and his wife's sister. He also had two children, a son 14 or 15 years old, and a daughter about 20. They were both living at home.

The next day a woman came to Pannek's and told us that the Germans had surrounded the town. They were ordering all the Jews to assemble in the market square. She had met my sister Eudel in a field outside of town. She told my sister to run and hide, but my sister said her parents were home all alone and that she must go back to them. And so my sister returned to the town.

The following day Pannek's sister-in-law went into the town to find out what had happened. She returned and told me that all the Jews were being held in the church, and the Germans were ordering all those Jews still in hiding to come out. My parents and one sister were with the other Jews, but one of my sisters was still hiding in the attic of my neighbor's house. It was my sister Fay. She was sick, and my father took her over to the neighbors. He didn't want her taken by the Germans while she was ill. There were rumors that the Germans were killing the sick right away.

The neighbor who was hiding my sister was very scared and wanted her to either go to the church with the other Jews or go into hiding with me. The next day I paid Pannek's sister-in-law 50 marks to smuggle my sister out of the town and bring her to me.

Pannek's sister-in-law dressed Fay up as a field hand going to work in the fields outside of town. Fay was very sick when she brought her. She was running a fever. When she saw me she started crying and banging her head against the wall. She kept saying that we should go with our parents. That we would not survive anyway. The Germans had put up notices that they would shoot any Jews they found, and they would also shoot any Poles that helped a Jew hide. But I said, "No, we would not go by ourselves into their hands," and I dragged her up to the attic.

For the next few days the Germans kept the Jews in the church. A few of the Jews who were still in hiding were caught. Some had given themselves up. Then all the Jews were taken to Wielun. I had a terrible feeling that the three of us were the only Jews left in the entire district.

Leipush was in the church with the other Jews. After the war he told me about a heated discussion between my father and my Uncle Lewi. Uncle Lewi was my mother's sister's husband.

After hearing what was happening to the Jews caught by the Germans my father wanted to tell the authorities where Fay and I were hiding. He still did not believe that he was going to die. Fortunately, my uncle talked him out of it. Uncle Lewi had a premonition about their fate and begged my father to wait until they knew more about the Germans' plans for them.

From Wielun the able bodied Jews were sent to Lodz, to labor in the ghetto. Leipush and Itzhak Moshe were among them. My sister Eudel could have gone with them but again would not leave my parents. After the war I learned of their fate. My sister, my parents, all my uncles, aunts, their families, and the other Jews from our town were made part of a larger group of Jews from the surrounding towns. On August 22, 1942 that group, almost 10,000 people, were sent to their deaths at a camp called Chelmno. At Chelmno the killing was done by gas van. The people were loaded into the van and the back doors sealed. The engine exhaust was directed into the sealed van as it moved.

Fay's illness was getting worse. Late at night I took her into town to see the doctor. The doctor was a Ukraneian named Taran. He was a very fine man. We knocked at his door, and I'm sure we woke him up. He let us in and examined Fay. He gave her some medicine that made her better. He refused to take any money from us saying we would need it more than he would.

As we were leaving, Dr. Taren said, "Go hide in small villages. There you will find less anti-Semitism than in the cities." We thanked him and left.

Later, toward the end of the war, as the Russian army approached our town, some of the townspeople attacked a group of Germans. In revenge the Germans shot and killed the leading citizens. Dr. Taran was among those killed.

Also among the townsmen killed in reprisal with Dr. Taran was the local butcher, Leon Schoch. Leon used to come and visit Pannek, and he spotted us hiding there. He wasn't known as a nice man, but since he hated the Germans, I knew he would not turn us in. In fact he offered to hide us, but I was afraid of him and of what he might do. He once said that he imagined that at the end of the war only he would have a Jewess, since the Germans would have killed off all the rest.

The first Saturday we were there, Pannek invited us to eat with his family in the house. Before that we ate all our meals in the stall's attic. The family tried to make the Sabbath a little nicer for us, but we were so depressed that Fay and I did little else but cry.

Pannek was too scared to hide us near the house during the day. Since a lot of people came to his house he was afraid we would be seen. During the day, when it wasn't raining, he told us to hide in the nearby fields. It was harvest time. The wheat was cut, bundled into stacks, and left standing in the fields to dry. The bundles of wheat gave us a lot of places to hide. We would leave the stall early in the morning. In the evening we would come back to the stall and go hide in the attic.

Once when we were hiding in the field we heard someone coming. We crawled into a stack of wheat. I looked out and saw 2 women walking towards us. It was Mrs. Yakobovich and her daughter, Estarka. Estarka was about 20 years old. They were neighbors of ours before the war.

I called their names. They came over. We hugged and cried. They said they were going to the Jewish ghetto in Czestochowa, because they had no place else to go. Mrs. Yakobovich wanted us to go with her, but I refused. I wanted them to stay with us, but they didn't want to hide anymore. So we said good-bye, and they went to Czestochowa. After the war Estarka told me what happened to them there.

As soon as they got into the ghetto the Germans caught them. First they were held with a group of other Jews. Then the Germans separated out the old people. The young they allowed to remain in the ghetto. As Mrs. Yakobovich was being taken away, she yelled to her daughter to run, to try to get away from the ghetto, and hide. Estarka got out and got to village a few kilometers from our home. The village was in a part of Poland that was German before the First World War. It had been cleared of Jews three years earlier. There she was able to hide out with a Christian family until the end of the war.

While at Pannek's a woman named Mrs. Guren came there looking for a place to hide. She was from our town, and her husband was in the same labor camp as Alter. She was a few years older than me and didn't have anything with her. Pannek would not let her stay, so I gave her 100 marks hoping it would help her. The same thing happened a day later when a Mrs. Salamanovic came there too. She also had to leave, and I gave her some money. I think it was 50 marks. Fay got very angry at me for giving away so much money. She screamed at me that I had a child and didn't know what we'd be facing. She was right, of course, but I had to do something for those ladies.

In a house next to Pannek lived a Pole who was known to be collaborating with the Germans. At night when we returned from the field we had to walk past this neighbor's yard. He had a dog and when we passed the dog would bark. This was one of the things that frightened Pannek, and every day he got more frightened. One day Pannek said that we would have to leave. He was too afraid to hide us any longer.

The next day I returned to the town to see one of the secretaries who worked in the town's city hall. With the town's Jews gone, one of his jobs now was to dispose of their property. He lived in the house next to mine. From him I hoped to get Polish papers for Fay and myself. I had heard that he arranged for forged papers for a price.

When I got to town I first went to my apartment to see if there was anything left. As I was walking into the building I was spotted by a neighbor. She looked at me but said nothing as she hurried out of the building. I found nothing in the apartment. It had been picked clean. I left and went to the secretary's house. I knocked on his door. As soon as he let me in we saw two policemen run into my apartment building. I knew it was the neighbor who told them of seeing me in the building. The secretary knew that it was me they were looking for.

The secretary made he hide until the police left. If I was caught in his house it would have cost him his life. As soon as they were gone he made me leave. He would not listen for a moment to what I wanted. He just shoved me out the door. I returned to Pannek's empty handed.

Pannek's wife was truly a wonderful human being. She pleaded with her husband to let us stay. After he repeatedly said no, she asked if she could set up a place for us in the barn. The barn was a little ways removed from the house and stall. She told him that she would do all that had to be done for us. That her husband would not even know we were there. But still he said no. So after two weeks of hiding at Pannek's we were sent away.

We went to a village near Wojcin. Wojcin was the town my mother was born in. We went to a family that had done business with my father. In the house lived an old woman with her daughter and son-in-law. The old woman had gone to school with my mother. She asked us why we didn't bring our mother with us. She would have helped her hide too.

We stayed there a short while hiding in their attic. One day two Germans came into their yard. Both the old woman's daughter and I saw them come in. We got very frightened. I was sure that someone had told on us until I saw they had bicycles and one was broken. They stopped to fix it and then went on their way.

We had such a bad fright that a few days later Fay noticed a patch of hair on my head had turned white. The young woman was pregnant then. She had been married for five years and this was going to be her first child. A few days after we had seen the Germans come into the yard she lost the child. It may have been because of the fright she had. The next day the husband came up to the attic and told us we would have to leave. He was very sorry about it, but they felt that they couldn't keep us anymore.

From there we went to another village called Drzdskowitz, to a Christian farmer named Urbonek. My husband knew him from doing business with him and felt he was a good man. My husband wrote that if I had to hide I should go to this man's house, tell him who I was, and he would surely let me hide there.

When I got there I found out that Urbonek was a leader in the village, appointed by the Germans. We came to his house at night. He let us in, gave us some food, and took us up to the attic.

Urbonek was in his middle 20s. He had a wife and some young children. His wife was very scared to have us in the house. We would sometimes hear them arguing about us being there. Since he was working for the Germans some of them would come to the house. Also they had a lot of enemies in the village because of the work they were doing. His wife was afraid of us being found there. It would have cost them their lives if we were.

Once I heard him say to his wife that if he was destined to die, he would, whether he was hiding Jews or not. But his wife prevailed and we were sent away. After the war I found out that he survived the war but was killed by the Poles for collaborating with the Germans.

On one of the days that we were at Urboneks', Nunyala was looking out the attic window. There were some children playing in front of the house. She wanted to go out and play with them. I told her she could not and tried to explain why. But she was still a young child and did not understand. All she knew was that she could not go out and play. She cried and pleaded with me to let her go outside. I still remember her asking me, when she stopped crying, "Mommy, why do I have to be Jewish?"

Many times she asked questions about what was happening to us and why. I can't forget those questions from my child for which I had no answers. Nunyala often talked about us making a big party when we went home, and everyone came home too, especially her father.

Urbonek sent us to his brother in another village, but they were also afraid. As soon as we came to their door Urbonek's sister-in-law started yelling that the village was surrounded, and that the Germans were looking for us. None of this was true, but the woman was hysterical. We could not stay there. They sent us somewhere else.

For a time we were just sent from village to village. A Christian once said to me, "Why do you risk our lives? No Jews will survive anyway."

In one place we came to, as soon as we walked in, the man there said that he was sure we were spotted and made us leave right away. Another place we came to late at night. We were allowed to stay the night but no more. In the morning we had to leave. After a while there was no place for us to go, so we decided we had to go to the Jewish ghetto in Czestochowa.

We went to another village, named Toplin. It was the village in which Alter was born. Toplin was 28 kilometers from Boleslawiec. There we went to a Christian named Antos Krzyzos. He was the same man who took the money to my cousin in Wielun when I tried to rescue my husband.

Antos was in his forties, on the thin side, and of average height. He raised poultry that Alter bought and also did odd jobs for Alter and Leipush.

As soon as we came to his house we told him we only wanted to stay for a short while. We told him of our wanting to get into the ghetto. Antos' family tried talking him out of letting us stay. They were afraid. But he said he would help us and took us up to the attic.

We couldn't just walk into the ghetto. If we were caught outside we would be shot. We had to be smuggled into it. I had a cousin in the ghetto named Rachel Liss. Rachel ran away from Wielun when her husband was taken away to labor camp. I knew that she had ended up in the Czestochowa ghetto. Antos helped me get a letter to her. We were taking a chance writing a letter to someone in the ghetto. If the Germans had read the letter we would have been caught, but Antos agreed to take the chance.

In the letter I asked her to find out how we could get into the ghetto. This was in September 1942. It was on Rosh Hashanah, the Jewish New Year, that we sent the letter. We spent the holiday up in the Krzyzos' attic. Two weeks later a letter came back from my cousin.

My cousin told us to go to the Ponow woods. The Ponow woods were near Wielun. There we would find a man whose name I can't remember now. She said that this man could smuggle us into the ghetto.

The next day we said good-bye to Antos Krzyzos and headed for the Ponow woods. We walked all day until we got to the woods. I remember it was a beautiful day. A number of Poles spotted us for Jews as we traveled there. Some were kind to us; some were not; but none of them turned us in. One told us that just the day before we came there the Germans had finished a large operation. For 2 weeks they searched the woods for Jews. Over 30 were caught hiding there. The Germans took them all to Wielun where they were all executed.

We came to the man my cousin told us see. He said that he could not get us into the ghetto anymore. Once he used to lead animals into the ghetto to be slaughtered for food. Then he was able to smuggle someone in by dressing them up as a helper. But the Germans stopped letting meat into the ghetto since they started taking Jews out of there. They wanted to make life more uncomfortable so it would be easier to get people to leave. So he was ordered not to come anymore.

A neighbor of his saw us come in. He stood outside the door and overheard us say we wanted to get into the ghetto. He offered to smuggle us in. We paid him about 300 marks, and that evening we went with him into the woods.

He led us around for about 4 hours. Once when I got tired of carrying my daughter and asked to rest he said we could not stop and he carried her for a while. Suddenly, he handed the child back to me and started running. Fay started running after him shouting for him to come back. I said for her to stop calling him and be thankful he just robbed us and didn't harm us as well.

It was dark, and we didn't know where we were so we laid down on the ground to wait for the sunrise. The ground was wet so I laid my daughter on top of me so she wouldn't catch a cold. She had slept through the whole thing.

In the morning we were able to see a village in the distance. We went there, and we looked for a house that was run down. We knew that the people living in poor houses were not Germans or collaborating with them.

We came into a house. We told the people the truth about who we were and what had happened to us. They said not to fear. They would talk to the village priest, and he would know what to do. The priest there was a very fine man. He advised that we go to the city of Klobuck, which was not far from there. There were still some Jews in Klobuck. One of them was the dentist. We were to go to the dentist, and he'd be able to help us get into a Jewish work camp nearby.

The dentist's name was Frankel. When we came into his office in Klobuck we found a group of SS officers sitting in his waiting room. They were waiting to have their teeth fixed. One of the Germans called the dentist out and asked him if he knew us. When the dentist saw us he literally turned white, but said that he did know us.

It turned out that Dr. Frankel had grown up in Wielun. I remembered my father talking about him. They went to school together. We told him our name was Liss, the daughters of an old friend of his. He said he remembered our father and would help us. After he was finished with the officers he got a Jewish young man to smuggle us into the work camp, which was a kilometer outside of Klobuck.

4
RUNNING

The camp outside Klobuck was called Podgorz. It was relatively easy to get in and out of the camp since it was lightly guarded, and the guards themselves were Jewish. We just walked up to the gate. The young man who Dr. Frankel sent along as our guide spoke to the guard, and we were let in.

While getting in was easy, staying there was not. The head of the work camp was a Jew from the city of Sosnowiec named Reuven Finer. He wanted us to go and register ourselves with the Gestapo. It was dangerous for the camp for unregistered Jews to be found there.

At that time a lot of Jews were running away from the ghetto in Czestochowa. Conditions in the ghetto were getting worse, and the Germans were starting to send them away from there. Some came to hide in Podgorz. The Jewish authorities in the camp arranged for a large group of them to be registered with the Germans.

The camp was made up of a few buildings. There were a few hundred adults in the camp, but no children. Children were not allowed to remain in the work camp. Even Reuven Finer could not keep his children in the camp. He had to leave them with his wife in the ghetto at Sosnowiec. Since I would not be parted with Nunyala, I refused to be registered. I made arrangements to leave the camp since the Jewish authorities there would not allow Nunyala to remain there in hiding. We decided that my sister Fay should stay there since we felt she would be safe. So Fay went with the others to be registered with the Gestapo.

We met an elderly Jew there named Zife. His daughter was the camp doctor and his son one of the camp administrators. He was such a fine man; may he rest in peace; he promised me he would look after Fay once I had left. He also helped get forged passports for my daughter and me.

A young man in the camp named Cholpack, who was from Wielun, forged for us two Polish passports. I didn't have much money to pay him so I gave him a good overcoat I had for him to sell. Instead of Goldrat, on the passport I was called Guntash, which was a Polish Christian name. With this passport I figured to get to Germany and find some work there.

At that time I thought that Germany would be the safest place to be. The war was going on in Russia and we heard that the fighting there was frightful. The rest of the continent was under strict German control. With so many people in the army there was a shortage of workers in Germany. Since I could speak German and had Polish papers I figured that hiding there might be easier than hiding in Poland.

It was now October 1942.

People in the camp advised me not to go to Germany. Winter was coming, they said, and it would be hard to move around to find work, especially since I did not know my way around there. Food was being rationed in Germany, and without ration cards we would have trouble getting anything to eat. I was told that the best thing to do was to try to find someplace to hide till spring and then try to get to Germany. After the winter there would be a need for field workers because of the spring planting. Then a woman and a child would not attract as much attention.

My sister and I said our good-byes, and I left the camp with my daughter. We started walking in the direction of our hometown. I thought it would be easier to hide there. Maybe even at Pannek's house again.

After the war I found out that the day we left the camp the Germans caught a Jewish woman and a child hiding nearby. They were shot and killed. When the news reached the camp Fay and everybody else thought it was us. There was a lot of recrimination over forcing a woman and child to leave. While Fay mourned us people argued over how we should have been helped rather than sent away. It was two years later that Fay learned that I was still alive.

Fay met Mrs. Guren in Podgorz. She was the lady who came to Pannek's house looking for a place to hide. She paid Fay back the 100 marks I gave her. Mrs. Guren did not survive long in that labor camp. A short while later she died of a heart attack.

Fay remained in Podgorz for about a year. Then she was transferred, with the rest of the camp, to a place called Longinbillo, which was near Breslau in Germany. Fay remained in Longinbillo working in a factory for the rest of the war.

We started walking home. Along the way we walked past a clothing factory. Both Nunyala and I were very hungry. We walked into the factory and approached the manager. I told him that I had a lot of experience sewing, and he gave me a job. But we only stayed there for a day. Too many Germans came into the factory. The town that was on my forged passport was nearby, and I was afraid I would be discovered. So we left.

It was early the next morning when we got to Pannek's. As soon as I got there I ran out of luck. As we walked into

Pannek's house, out walked Leon Schoch. He was very happy to see me. After he left Pannek said, "Girl, you can't stay here because Leon will want you to go with him, and if you won't he will surely threaten to tell the Germans."

I knew he was right and that I would have to leave the area.

Before I left I asked Pannek if he would keep my daughter there over the winter. I offered to pay him. If Nunyala stayed with him I wouldn't have to fear for her so much. I could go back to the work camp where I left my sister and stay there for the winter. In the spring I would come back for Nunyala, and together we would go to Germany.

Pannek said, "Go up to the attic and hide from your daughter, and we'll see if she would get used to it here."

But she carried on for such a long time that Pannek finally said, "Even if you give me a room full of gold I could not keep your child."

After that Nunlaya was so afraid I would leave her that she had to go with me everywhere I went. She would often put her arms around my neck and say, "Mommy, you would never give me away, would you?"

We went to stay with other Christians I knew, but it was like before. They were too afraid to keep us very long and would soon send us away.

Not far from Pannek lived Urbonek's sister. Her name was Marisha. She lived with her father-in-law. Her husband was in a labor camp in Germany. We went to her house.

The father-in-law was afraid to let us stay there and told Marisha to get rid of us, but she said, "No, it's Saturday, and they should at least stay the Sabbath."

I showed them my passport thinking that would change her father-in-law's mind, but Marisha said it would do me no good in Boleslawiec. I was too well known. She was, of course, right. I told her I did not know what else to do or where else to go. She suggested I go to the Protectorat. There the passport would do us some good. Maybe there we could find somewhere to stay and wait till spring.

The Germans split off the eastern part of Poland, the part I lived in, and administered it from Germany. The western part of the country was given to Russia as part of a treaty with Germany at the beginning of the war. The middle part of the country was under a Polish government set up by the Germans. This area was called the Protectorat or the General Gouvernement. The Germans set up a border between the eastern and the middle parts of Poland. The border was guarded as if they were two separate countries.

To get to the Protectorat we had to be smuggled across the border. Marisha knew of some people who had arranged to have them selves smuggled across the border. She went to find how they did it.

When she returned she said that Nunyala and I should go to the city of Gnashin. We would be able to get there by train. In Gnashin, which was near the General Gouvernement border, I could find a smuggler to get us across.

I knew that it was no easy thing to get across the border, but I had no choice. I had to try.

On Sunday morning Nunyala and I set out for the train station. On the way I spotted two policemen walking toward us at a distance. I froze in my tracks. I recognized the two of them and knew that if they looked at me they would recognize me too. I didn't know what to do. If I ran or suddenly turned around it would surely attract their attention. If I stayed they would see me as well.

Suddenly, before I had a chance to do anything, a woman who I never saw before in my life, rode up next to us in her wagon. She said to me, "Quickly, get in."

We got in, and she rode us past the policemen. As we passed them she blocked their view of me. But they did not notice anything, and we got to the station safely. As I got off the wagon I asked her how she knew I was in danger. She smiled and said that she just knew. Then she rode away. Standing there looking at her go I had a strange feeling. Could I have been looking at an angel? I don't know, but to this day I think it might have been.

At the station I met a couple that lived in my apartment building. They came over and told me how sad they were at what was happening to me. They knew I was running and hiding, and they wished me luck.

As I waited for the train I overheard a Polish girl talking to a well-dressed German woman. Pointing to me she said that I was Jewish and that she knew me from the town. I heard the German woman say to her, "Let her go. She has a child with her."

We were unmolested as we boarded the train.

When we got to Gnashin, which was just a kilometer from the border, it was raining and cold. My daughter was shivering, and I had no place to go. I saw some Germans in the street outside the train station so we just walked into a house nearby.

The people in the house asked me who I was, and what I wanted. I asked them if we might stay the night. I showed them my Polish passport and made up a story about my husband being wanted by the Germans for killing a pig. It was against the ration laws to kill a pig without approval. The penalty was death. So my husband ran away, and I also had to run away. I told them I was trying to get across the border.

They didn't believe me at all and told me to get out of their house. They said if I wasn't a Jew, certainly my child was, and drove us out of the house.

I walked across the street and walked into another house. The man there was very nice. He saw my daughter was wet and cold, and he told us to come in and sit down. He gave us something warm to drink. His wife was sick and in bed, and he had a 20 year old daughter living there. Again I showed my passport and told the same story about my husband killing a pig. They said we could stay the night.

The man's daughter asked me what I would do when I got across the border. I told her I would look for a job as a seamstress since I could sew. She said that she needed a seamstress and that she had a sewing machine. She asked me to stay awhile and sew for her. The place was warm, and there was food, so I happily said I would stay. I, of course, was in no rush to go anywhere so I thought myself very lucky. For the next two days I did some sewing for the family.

On the second day, as I was sitting out in the yard, I saw a neighbor looking at me out his window. He stared at me for a long while. That evening as I sat at the sewing machine the young girl came and sat down next to me. I noticed that she was shaking. I feared that someone had said something to her, so I got an idea.

She had a brother who worked in the coalmines in a nearby town. Every few nights he came home. I asked her if he was coming home that night. She said he was, and I asked if she thought he would send a letter for me from the next town. I said that I wanted to let my parents know that I was all right, but I didn't think it safe to post it from Gnashin.

She brought me a post card and a pen. She sat near me as I wrote out the card. I started the card with a greeting that the Christians used when they wrote. When I finished the card I gave it to her to give to her brother.

As I knew she would she read the card because a short while later she came back into the room, smiling. She told me that the neighbor who had spied me from his window was a policeman and had said to her that I was a Jew. She told him that I was not, and now the card proved it. We both laughed about it, but on the inside I was quite scared. I knew that I would have to leave as soon as I could.

I really did not know where to go. In the time I was there I had not inquired on how to get across the border. I was now 14 kilometers from Klobuck where I had left my sister. I decided to try the camp at Klobuck again. Maybe Fay would be able to hide us or get us into a ghetto somewhere.

The next morning I got up early and watched as the policeman left his house. I told the family I was staying with that in Klobuck I had friends that I wanted to see before I went across the border. I told them I would return and asked for directions to Klobuck.

They told me to take a road that circled half way around the town. We were to stay on that road until we got to a large gate. From there the road straightened out and went straight to Klobuck. We said good-bye, and left. Along the way it started raining. We walked until we came to a large gate, and there the road split in two.

I stood there for a while not knowing which road to take. Then a wagon rode up and stopped. I greeted the man on the wagon with a greeting that Christians used when they said hello to each other. He gave me a very mean look. He must have spotted me for a Jew. I pointed down one of the roads and asked if that was the way to Klobuck. He very angrily answered me, "Yes," and quickly rode off.

We started walking down that road. We walked for a long time till we got to a village. Outside the village were big warning signs, but since it was raining and my daughter was cold, we just hurried past them. Later, I remembered it said that we were entering the General Gouvernement area. But since I thought we were going to Klobuck, I didn't stop to look at the signs.

I didn't know where I was. So I walked up to a house along the road and asked some people standing outside. The people at the house asked what did I mean where was I. They said that I had just crossed the border into Czestochowa. In trying to go to Klobuck I accidentally crossed into the Protectorat.

The people asked why nobody stopped me at the border. I said I saw no one there. Just as we were talking a police car went by and took up a position along the border. The people said that not for one minute since 1939 was the border left unguarded until today.

At first I was going to go to the ghetto in Czestochowa. I thought I might find someone I knew, maybe someone from my town. I wanted desperately to see a familiar face. On the way there I saw a column of Jews being led by some German soldiers. I found out that this was happening every day. The Germans were removing the ghetto's inhabitants. So I changed my mind.

I decided to go to Ostrow Lubelski near Lublin. Lublin was on the eastern side of the General Gouvernement. There I hoped to find my oldest brother, Gavriel, and his family. I had not heard from them in a long time, but since the Germans had resettled them there I thought they might still be there.

We went to the train station in Czestochowa and bought a ticket to Lublin. The ticket seller asked me which way I wanted to go since there was no direct train to Lublin. He asked if I wanted to go through Kielce or Warsaw. I asked which way was better. He said to go through Warsaw. That train was due to arrive in Warsaw at 9:00 P.M., and the train to Lublin left there two hours later at 11:00. So we took the train to Warsaw.

5
WARSAW

The train traveled very slowly. At times it just pulled over onto a siding and sat for what seemed like hours. We pulled into Warsaw after 11:00 P.M. and missed the train to Lublin. We sat in the train station all night. The next train to Lublin didn't leave till 7:00 in the morning.

As we sat waiting for the morning train a lady sat down next to us. She was tall, thin, middle-aged, and dressed like a peasant. She asked where we were going. I said to Lublin. She said she was going there too and would help me with my packages. I had two packages with me.

While waiting, Nunyala started talking about home and started naming some of the members of our family. The woman heard her talking and must have known we were Jewish.

In the morning they called out the track from which the train to Lublin would be leaving. The woman asked me to wait and watch her bag. She said she had to go to the toilet. Within a few minutes she returned. I took Nunyala's hand in one hand and one of my packages in the other. The women picked up her bag and my other package, and together we started walking to the train for Lublin.

We went down a flight of stairs, and at the bottom a Polish policeman stopped me. The woman continued walking with my package. I asked the policeman why he stopped me, and he said that the women I was with said that I was a Jew. I said to him, "See why she said I was a Jew. It's my package she is carrying, and while you keep me here, she's running off with it."

I showed him my passport and said it was the other woman he should be detaining because she was a thief.

He didn't listen to me and took a very long look at my passport. For a Jew in Warsaw to be outside the ghetto was against the law, and could bring them the death penalty. An elderly German came over and asked the policeman what was the matter. He said that he was told that I was a Jew. The German told me to follow him.

He took us to a German police station next to the train station. At the police station another German started questioning me in German. I understood German, as did all Jews since Yiddish was so similar to it, but I made believe that I didn't understand a word he said. He asked me what I was, Jewish or Polish, as he looked over my passport. I kept saying I was Polish. The German who brought me in then said to the other one that he thought that I was Polish. They handed me back my passport and let us go.

I returned to the train station and again was stopped by the same Polish policeman. He asked why the Germans let me go. I told him that they saw that I was a Pole. Since my papers were in order they let me go. He then told me to come with him to the Polish police station. As he took me there he said, "Poles can tell better than the Germans who is a Jew."

Where he took me I didn't know. I had never been in Warsaw before. The police station was a large room with an iron gate dividing it in the middle. As soon as we walked in my daughter said, "Mommy, this looks like the Gemeinde at home."

The Gemeinde was the building that housed the Jewish community organization. The policeman heard her say this and said to me, "Do you still say you're not Jewish?"

I said that we were not Jewish but that my daughter played with Jewish children at home and knew what their community center looked like.

They put us in a jail cell full of women, some of whom I learned, were prostitutes. We stayed there all night. Some of the other women bothered me, but I ignored them.

The cell was in a large room with bars down the middle. One side was for the women and the other for the men. As I sat near the bars separating the room I saw a young man walk over to the bars near me. He looked around making sure nobody was listening. With his head and hand he motioned for me to come closer. He looked Jewish so I went over to him. When I got near him he whispered, "Amcha?" Hebrew for our nation.

I answered, "Yes," also in Hebrew. He asked me how I got there, and I told him my story.

I asked him what had happened to him. He said that he had escaped from Treblinka and was caught outside the ghetto. I had heard of Treblinka before, but did not know much about it. I asked him what was in Treblinka.

First he told me about the trains from Warsaw. How the people were loaded like cattle. When they arrived at Treblinka the living were made to leave the train. The dead were carried off. The people were made to line up, men to one side, women to the other. They were ordered to undress, and then led into the gas chamber. After they were dead, Jewish young men were used to carry out the bodies.

He told me how he had escaped from Treblinka. His work there was to load the trains with the belongings of the Jews that had died from the previous transport. Once when the

German guards weren't looking, he hid between some of the bundles packed into the boxcar. The train carried him out of the camp. While it was moving he jumped and came back to Warsaw. He was caught before he got back into the ghetto.

I was going to ask him why he came back, but before I could, some other people moved near us. He stopped talking and moved away. Shortly before the uprising I saw this young man again in the ghetto. I did not have a chance to speak with him, but I found out that he was with the partisans.

That night I could not sleep. I kept hearing his words over and over again.

The next morning a policeman came in, ordered my daughter and me to collect our things, and follow him. We were led into a small room and searched from head to foot. Anything of value that was found on us was taken away. Then we were led us outside. I thought they were going to shoot us. We were led through a gate, and as soon as we passed the gate I saw a policeman with a white armband with a blue Jewish star on it. Then I knew we were being taken into the ghetto and not to be shot.

As I traveled to Warsaw I had overheard people talking about the ghetto. They were saying that there was no more ghetto. That the Germans had already taken everyone out. That the Jews from Warsaw were all killed by the Germans. But after I saw that Jewish policeman I knew there was still a Jewish ghetto and thanked God that I was among Jews again.

We entered the ghetto from Niska Street. We walked for a few blocks until we got to a building on Gesia Street. The building was a prison called the Gesiowka. We were led inside and again put in a cell full of women.

I still refused to speak anything but Polish and still did not admit to being Jewish. The other women in the cell laughed at me and said they had done the same thing. That I wasn't fooling anyone now that I was among other Jews. Everyone also said that in a few days they were going to take all the Jews they had caught outside the ghetto to Treblinka.

In prison everyone talked about where they were hiding and how they got caught.

One girl told me that she was with a Polish family, and the husband tried to take advantage of her. His wife got jealous and chased her out of the house.

Another girl, Yagha Gold, who later became a friend, told of hiding in a hotel used by prostitutes. She had a Polish young man who loved her and paid to hide her there. One day the police raided the hotel and found her hiding in her room. By the way she looked and dressed they knew she was no prostitute and suspected that she was Jewish.

Another young girl in our cell told a horrifying tale. She had come from Vilna, a city in the northeast of Poland. One day the Germans gathered all the Jews and marched them to a field outside of the city. The Jews were forced to dig a large pit. They were made to undress. Then they were lined up, in groups, in front of the pit and shot with a machine gun. As they were shot they fell into the pit.

The young girl was in one of the last groups shot. In the middle of the night she woke up in the pit full of bodies. She crawled out and by moonlight found some rags. She put them on and ran into the woods. At the first house she came to she knocked. The Poles there were too frightened to hide her but gave her some food and clothing. She made her way to Warsaw where she had some family, but was caught before she could get into the ghetto.

We stayed in prison for about 8 days. During that time a lot of Jews were caught on the outside of the ghetto and brought to the prison. There was a lot of talk in prison about the Poles making an uprising against the Germans on the 11th of November. The 11th was the anniversary of the establishment of Poland after World War 1. We were sure there would be an uprising, and we would all be set free.

In our prison cell there were over 300 women. The cell was 10 feet wide and about 40 feet long. The floor was of rough stone and very cold. Along the sides of the two long walls were benches where the people could sit and lie down to sleep. We all ate in this crowded cell. Once a day we were let out into a yard, for a short while, to get some air.

The cell was getting so crowded that there wasn't enough room for everybody to sleep on the benches at the same time. Those people who were in prison the longest didn't want to share the benches with the newcomers. The whole group split into two factions. I was among the newcomers who argued that the benches had to be shared. I once yelled at two women who were arguing with each other. At the top of my voice I said, "Hitler doesn't have to kill us. We could do it very well ourselves."

Among the women in the prison there were 6 with children. One day some women who worked for the ghetto's Judenrat came and asked us to give them the children. They had a small children's home set up in the ghetto. They asked us to give them the children so they could be better cared for. They told us that there was more food for them in the home and since they didn't know what would happen to us, it would be better if they had the children. They didn't want to tell us that we were most likely going to be executed, and by giving them the children the children would be spared. But none of the children would go. My daughter started crying as soon as I mentioned it to her. She grabbed me around the neck and would not let go. None of the children would let themselves be taken from their mothers. So none of them went.

It was now November 1942 and our eighth day in prison. In the middle of the day some Germans came in and ordered all the women and children to get out. They had us line up in rows in the prison courtyard. We thought that they were sending us away to Treblinka. A group of Germans stood in front of us and made a couple of speeches. One of them was a tall, thin SS officer. Later I learned that his name was Konrad. They told us that they were issuing a general pardon to everyone in prison. They were issuing it because the Vichy government in France had formally allied themselves with the Germans. In celebration they were releasing us and sparing us our lives.

Until this time the French were officially neutral. On the 8th of November the Allies invaded French North Africa. This angered the Vichy government, and they joined the war on Germany's side.

One of the German officers told us to follow him. As we were led through the ghetto a man came over to us and said in Yiddish, "Jews, dance. Sing." He started dancing and clapping his hands. "You had been sentenced to death, but by a miracle your lives were spared. Before today all the Jews caught outside the ghetto walls were sent to Treblinka."

None of us felt like singing or dancing.

We were taken to a buiiding on Niska Street, near the Umschlagplatz. Umschlagplatz was the German word for loading place. It was the rail yard where the Jews were loaded into boxcars for the trip to Treblinka.

Niska Street was where the work details assembled. There was a kitchen set up, and we were given some food. When we were done eating we were lined up for a selection.

The old people among us were taken away. The young women, even the ones with children, were picked for various work details.

A card with a number was hung around my neck. The card was called an Ausweise. It said I belonged to a detail called the Werterfassung. Werterfassung, in German, meant collection of valuables. The Werterfassung was an SS run enterprise in the ghetto.

With this card the Germans considered my presence in the ghetto as legal. They declared it illegal for a Jew to remain in the ghetto unless they were there working for the Germans. There were still people living and hiding in the ghetto who did not have cards. They were called the Wild Ones. If caught by the Germans they would be taken to prison. Sometimes they were shipped off to Treblinka. Most of the time they were just shot.

We were told to report for work in the morning. That day we were to form groups of 4, and together we would be given an apartment in the ghetto. In prison I got to know 3 other women. Their names were Sala and Genia Buter, they were sisters, and a friend of theirs Yagha Gold. Yagha was the one I mentioned that was caught hiding in a Warsaw hotel. We were on the same side in prison concerning the benches. They took me into their group, and together we were given an apartment.

The apartment was in the section of the ghetto set aside for the people who were working for the Germans. This section was now called the small ghetto.

Our apartment was at Muranowska 38. On one side of Muranowska 38 was number 36, which was burned out, and on the other side of the center courtyard was Neska 7. Across from Neska 7 was the soup kitchen for the workers.

We were given a room that was on the second floor. The room had one window overlooking the courtyard. The room was a mess. The walls had holes in them. There were broken plates on the floor and torn pillows with their feathers all about the room.

We were told about the large roundups of Jews that had gone on before we came. In all the buildings, in all the rooms, the SS searched for Jews. After removing them the soldiers searched for valuables. In their search they tore up everything. This is what had happened to our room.

In this one room we, 4 adults and 1 child, were to live. In our building lived over 100 Jewish families under these same crowded conditions.

In the basement of our building was a bakery. The other girls told Nunyala and me to go down and get some food while they cleaned up the room. In the bakery I met a lady who lived in the apartment across the hall from us. Her name was Mrs. Bshostek. She lived there with her 6 children. She was a widow. Most of her children were grown. Two of her children were married, and their spouses lived in the apartment, too.

The Bshosteks were from a small town near Warsaw called Powazek. All the Jews from the nearby towns were chased out of their homes and forced into the Warsaw Ghetto. Since we didn't have any bedding yet she invited my daughter and me to sleep that first night in her apartment. The three girls I was to share the room with spent that night in the bakery because we didn't have any wood yet to heat the room.

The next morning when the room was all cleaned up we went out searching for bedding and chairs. We brought back a couple pieces of furniture and put the place in order. Then we went to find out about the jobs to which we were assigned.

We returned to Neska 7, the assembly place for the work details. My daughter refused to stay in the apartment even though a neighbor said she would look after her. So she came to work with me.

That day was very cold, and it snowed. Nunyala was cold and hungry, but she was so afraid I would leave her she clung to me the whole time. I could not even go to the bathroom without her.

When I got to the assembly area a German asked me why I brought my daughter. I told him that just the day before I was released from prison and did not have any family to leave her with. I was excused from work that day and told to take my daughter to the children's home. The German said that the children got treated well there and that I would be able to visit her there in the evenings.

Nunyala asked me to tell her about this home. I told her it would be warm there. She would have more food, and that there would be other children to play with. I told her she would have to sleep there but that I would come and see her every day after work. Also on Saturdays, when I wouldn't have to work, she would be allowed to come and stay with me. She made me promise that I would come and see her every evening. I promised, and she asked me to take her to the children's home.

The home was in Zamenhof 56. It was called the Internat. When we came there some staff members asked me how we got to Warsaw. I told them our story. They cried with me, and they took in my child.

Nunyala was the 19th or 20th child there. At one time the home was very large. Once there were over 300 children there. The few children who remained were from the people who were still working in the ghetto.

The staff at the home was from Janusz Korczak's Children's Home. Janusz Korczak was internationally famous as a teacher and administrator of a home for Jewish orphans in

Warsaw. They told me the story of how the Germans took Korczak and his children out of the ghetto a few months before. The Germans offered Korczak his freedom, but he refused to abandon his children. The morning they were to leave he made sure the children were all clean and dressed. When the Germans came the children were lined up and ready. He walked in front of the children as they went to the train. The train took them all to Treblinka.

Every day after work I would come to see my daughter. One day at work I found a gold pin. I sold it to a Pole who worked among us but was able to come in and out of the ghetto. With the money I bought some extra food and brought it to my daughter.

In the evenings I stayed with her until it was time for the children to go to sleep. Then I would have to run to my apartment building so I would not get caught outside after curfew. Sometimes Nunyala would cry and hold onto me when I tried to leave. The nurses would threaten not to let me come anymore if she continued to carry on. She would then try to stop crying and would let me go.

The work I was assigned to was called the Werterfassung. The Werterfassung's job was to go from the smaller section of the ghetto, where we lived, into the larger section and help remove anything that the Germans could use. I still remember our group leader, a Jewish policeman named Bestermen.

Bestermen was tall and heavyset. I remember him as being good to me and to the others as well. Once he asked me to come live with him. The Jewish policemen lived in their own barracks with their families. He offered to arrange for my daughter to live with us too, but I turned him down. I told him that I knew that my husband was still alive and that I could not just live with a man that way. He said he understood and never mentioned it again.

Before November the Werterfassung had about 800 workers. Now they added another 800 workers to help clean out the ghetto.

During the summer of 1942 most of the Jews were removed from the ghetto forcibly. They left behind all of their belongings. This is what the Germans had us search through for anything of value.

There were only about 30,000 Jews still in the ghetto at that time. There were once half a million. The Germans were always shrinking the ghetto in what was called an Aktion. In an Aktion the SS would surround a group of blocks, search all the houses in those blocks, and take out of the ghetto all the Jews they found. Sometimes even people with work cards were taken. Then they would close off those blocks, and that's how they would shrink the ghetto.

By the time I arrived in Warsaw the ghetto had shrunk to about a dozen streets in the section I lived. There was also another occupied section in the center of the old ghetto. That one was 3 or 4 streets. It was for the brush makers. These people worked in the Toebben's shop and lived in the buildings nearby.

In groups of 45 to 50 we would go into the sections of the ghetto that had been cleared of people. We searched the houses and apartments for anything of value. All the clothing, all the furniture, anything that could be carried was brought to the courtyard of each building. There everything was loaded onto carts. Poles working for the Germans would lead the carts out of the ghetto. If we found anything small and valuable we would trade for it with these Poles.

Once during the search of an apartment one of the groups uncovered the hiding place of a woman and two children.

They were the ones we called Wild Ones because they had no papers that allowed them to stay in the ghetto. As soon as they were found the woman grabbed the children and started running. Some of the men ran after them trying to stop them from going out into the street. They shouted after them that we would not give them away, but the woman would not stop. She just kept running with the children.

From the window of the room I was working in, I saw them run out into the street. As soon as they left the building they attracted the attention of two SS soldiers standing nearby. The soldiers shouted for them to stop, but the woman and the children kept on running. The soldiers chased after them. The woman and children turned a corner, and I could not see them anymore. But when the soldiers got to the corner I saw one of them raise his machine gun and fire. I trembled at the sound of the gun, and heard the woman and children cry out. I didn't see the woman and children get shot, but I know they were. The soldiers just stood there for a few seconds and then calmly walked away.

A girl named Alla Dichtwald lived alone in our apartment building. She was 23 or 24 years old and also worked with me in the Werterfassung. She had no family in our section of the ghetto. Her mother and sister worked for Toebben and lived in a building near the shop.

After a few weeks the girls I was living with found some relatives of theirs living in another building. The relatives got them good jobs and had the girls move in with them. Alla knew that I was alone. She suggested that we move in together. At first I did not want to, but Alla always looked so bedraggled and unkempt that I took pity on her and let her move in with me. She was trying so hard to befriend me. I decided to pretend she was a sister and started looking after her. In a short while I was glad she was around. She helped ease my loneliness.

The Germans told us to write letters to our families telling them everything was all right with us. I wrote many letters wanting to tell someone that I was alive and where I was. I wrote home in case someone was there, though I knew nobody was. I wrote to my husband, my brothers, and sisters. I addressed the letters to where I had last heard they were. I never received any replies and don't know of anyone who ever received any of my letters.

During this time Fay and Alter were able to exchange letters. Alter was in a Lager named Guttenbron. A Lager was what we called a work camp. Guttenbron was near Posnan. I knew he never got my letters because Fay remembers him asking, in every one of his letters, if she had heard anything about me.

Sometime in the middle of December I made a deal with the man who ran the bakery in my building. Every morning I took from him 50 rolls. During a break at work I sold 40 of them to the people I worked with. The money I turned over to the baker. The remaining rolls I kept as payment. Two of them I ate. Two I gave to a girl who worked with us, named Chirmcha. She had lost her whole family and most of the time walked around in a daze. The rest of the rolls I took each night to my daughter.

One day near the end of the year, as I was walking out of the bakery with the 50 rolls, Bestermen, the Jewish policeman came over to me. He told me that a group of young men, who were with the partisans, were nearby and needed the bread. Would I give it to them? I said, "Yes."

Besterman took the bread and walked over to a sewer cover in the middle of the street. He looked around and then tapped on the cover. A young man lifted it from below and was handed the bag of rolls. He disappeared down the hole with the bag. Besterman put back the sewer cover. It was the first time I had seen a member of the partisans.

6
AKTIONS

Nunyala was able to stay with me on the weekends. There was no work on Saturday, so we would spend the day together. On Sunday I worked, but she stayed in the apartment and went back to the home Monday mornings. Sometimes she didn't want to go right back. So I would let her sleep late on Monday, and a neighbor would watch her during the day. When I came home from work Monday evening, I would return her to the home.

This went on from November 1942 till the middle of January 1943.

The nurses who watched the children at the Internat were the first to tell me about the Aktions the Germans conducted to round up Jews and take them out of the ghetto. The Aktions had stopped at the end of the summer, but it was only a matter of time before they started up again. The nurses told all the mothers that during an Aktion they should not come running to the home because they had a good hiding place for themselves and the children. They told us to arrange for our own hiding place and wait a few days for everything to settle down. Then when things returned to normal we could come to the home.

On Thursday evening, January 14, as I was coming home from work I went by Muranowska 40. A group of people stood around the entrance to the building. There stood a wagon, the kind of wagon used to take away a dead person. I asked someone what had happened, and he said that Rabbi Doctor Balaban had committed suicide.

Doctor Balaban worked for the ghetto's Judenrat. Before the war he was a famous historian. The Germans were forcing Dr. Balaban to give a speech that Saturday night to the Jews in the ghetto. As a Jewish leader, the Germans wanted him to tell everyone to cooperate with the Germans as they evacuated the ghetto. But instead of helping the Germans he took his own life.

We didn't know it then, but the Germans had a big Aktion planned for that Monday, January 18.

The evening Dr. Balaban died I went to see my daughter, as I did every evening. That day all the children were sick with a skin rash. They were being treated with a cream. I returned on Friday evening, and the nurses said that none of the children would be allowed to leave for the weekend.

I went to the home on Saturday and on Sunday to help with the children and just to be with Nunyala. When I left her on Sunday night I stopped in the hall outside the children's bedroom. I leaned against the wall and started to cry. I stayed there for over an hour, I just couldn't bring myself to leave. My heart ached as I looked at the children. I cried every time I saw my daughter lying there sick and in pain.

It was the last time I would see my child.

That Sunday night, January 17, when I got back to my apartment I heard that there was going to be an Aktion in the morning. Everybody was running around getting ready to go into hiding. Alla and I quickly gathered up some of our things and hurried to our hiding place.

On the street side our apartment building was 2 stories high. Around the center courtyard it was 4 stories high. The end of the hallways on the third and forth floors originally led to attics. The entrance to the attic on the third floor was made to look like a closet. So it appeared that the hallway now ended in a broom closet. In the closet was a small hidden door very low on the far wall. In front of the door stood a large garbage pail that completely covered the door. The pail was always kept full of garbage to discourage anyone from moving it and looking behind it. This small door was the entrance to a very large attic room. That was our hiding place. Over 100 Jews entered this room to hide from the SS on that Sunday night.

The room had no light, of course. A light would make it easier to find. Everyone brought what food they could with them. To go into hiding people prepared small packages of dried bread. I brought nothing with me, but people shared what little they had.

There was a crawlspace leading from the other side of the room to another building. The crawlspace was used as a toilet. Once in awhile some of the young men would go through the crawlspace into the next building. They would bring back news of what was happening in the ghetto.

All day Monday we could hear the soldiers in the street and in our building looking for us. When the Germans searched the building they found the attic on the fourth floor. They did not think of looking for another one on the third floor. Of course no one hid in the fourth floor attic. Our hiding place was an excellent one. Even during the following April's Aktion it was not discovered. Only during the uprising, when the building was set on fire, did the people finally have to abandon it.

By the evening I wanted to leave the hiding place and go to my daughter. The other people would not let me leave. They were afraid I would be caught and give the hiding place away.

The following evening I got out of the attic, but I could not get out of the building. On the first floor of our building was a shop that made uniforms for the Germans. The people working in the shop were left alone by the SS during this Aktion. Employees of companies doing work for the war were exempt from deportation. The shop people knew about our hiding place. They wouldn't let me leave because they had told the Germans that nobody was hiding in the building, and if I were caught leaving they could all be killed. The shop people chased me back into the hiding place.

On the third day of the Aktion it was a lot quieter on our street, and I was let out of the building. I ran to the children's home but found the children and the nurses gone. Because of the children's illness they did not make it to their hiding place. They were all taken away by the Germans.

I ran around looking for anybody who knew what had happened to the children. I found out that the Jewish undertaker had found a child in the street near the school and had taken the child home with him.

I ran to the undertaker's apartment and there saw one of the children from the home. He looked at me and said, "You are Nunya's mother."

I asked him how he got here and if he remembered anything of what had happened to the other children.

He said he remembered his mother coming into the home and quickly taking him and his sister out. As they ran along the street he looked back and saw his mother and sister fall, and then he fell. After that he woke up in the bed he was lying in and didn't remember anything else.

The undertaker told me what he thought had happened to the boy. It seemed that his mother came for her children at the start of the Aktion but was killed by the SS as she tried to run from them. The boy was knocked unconscious and left for dead. When the undertaker discovered that the boy was alive he brought him home.

I learned nothing else, until after the war, of what had happened to the children and to the women who watched them. All I knew was that they were gone.

At that time the Germans had planned that the Aktion would be the final liquidation of the ghetto, but there was some resistance by the Jews. It was a small uprising, and the resistance surprised the Germans. After three days they let it be known that it was just an Aktion and that it was over. They said that the ghetto would remain and that everybody should go back to work.

After the January Aktion the ghetto changed. The Juddenrat lost control to the young men and women who were the partisans. They called themselves the Jewish Fighting Organization. They were preparing for the final defense of the ghetto. Everyone knew that another uprising was coming. Some feared it because they knew that it would mean the final end of the ghetto.

Before Nunyala was taken away I had planned, with two of the other woman from work, to escape from the ghetto with my daughter. We were going to join the partisans outside of Warsaw. But it was very cold that January and because of my daughter we decided to wait until spring. Now that she was gone I didn't care anymore.

After the January Aktion I never saw those girls again. I don't know if they were caught during the Aktion or if they made it out of the ghetto.

Two men from our apartment house did get out of the ghetto at that time. Both men were without papers. Wild ones they were called. One of the men tried to get me to go along, but I would not go. They got into a work camp outside

Warsaw, but soon after they got there the camp was closed and everyone was sent to Lublin. I met them there when I got to Lublin a few weeks later. So we ended up in the same place anyway.

I lived in a state of despair. I went back to work, but I was heartbroken over my daughter. Nothing that happened around me interested me anymore. I lived this way until the uprising on April 19, 1943, the day before Passover.

In our apartment building lived a family named Kornblat. Their son was a policeman in the ghetto. On the morning of April 19th he came into the building and told everybody to go into the hiding place. He said that the Germans had surrounded the ghetto and were about to start an Aktion. This we knew was to be the last of the ghetto.

As we were hurrying to our hiding place we heard firing in the streets of the ghetto. People were saying that this was the uprising. That the shootings were from the Jewish partisans who had organized a defense of the ghetto.

From our hiding place we were able to see groups of Jews, with their hands in the air, being led down the street by the SS. I looked out between some boards onto Muranowska Street. I saw a group being led to the Umschlagplatz.

The shooting went on all day. In the evening it got very still in the ghetto.

In our hiding place, people talked about the uprising at the Toebben's shop and the Schultz factory. Among us 100 Jews there wasn't one gun. There was nothing to fight with. We were sure that the Poles would supply us with weapons once the uprising started, but nothing came.

As things quieted down outside our hiding place the building janitor, a very thin man, opened a bag and pulled out 2-dozen hard-boiled eggs. The janitor ran a small food store out of his apartment. We couldn't have been more surprised. All those eggs were worth a fortune at that time in the ghetto. He smiled as he looked at our faces and said, "I brought something for the Seder."

A normal Passover Seder we could not, of course, have. But in our current predicament the story of Passover gave us some hope. The eggs were cut in fours, and everybody got a quarter of an egg during the Seder.

There was a young couple among the hundred Jews in the hiding place. The woman was a pretty, blond haired lady named Malka. They had a baby that was only a few weeks old. The baby's grandmother was the woman who let my daughter and me stay in her apartment our first night in the ghetto. During the first night in hiding the baby cried often.

Every time the baby cried the other people would tell the parents to keep the baby quiet, but the parents could not keep it quiet for long. The more the baby cried the angrier the other people grew and the more frantic the parents became. We knew that the SS would be prowling the streets and buildings looking for the hiding places. We all had to walk slowly and talk only in whispers. The baby's crying put all of us in danger of being found.

In the morning the noise outside got louder. The SS had come back into the ghetto. This time they had tanks, and the shooting started once again. The noise started the baby crying, and the parents just could not stop it. A group of men told the young couple that they had to either leave the hiding place, give them the baby, or put it to sleep themselves.

They couldn't leave the hiding place. We were all sure that going out into the ghetto meant certain death, either from being shot on the street or from being sent to Treblinka. They also couldn't kill the baby themselves. The couple talked quietly together for a while. Then the husband took the baby from his wife and gave it to one of the other men. The husband sat back down next to his wife, and they started to cry.

The men took the baby to the other side of the room. The group of men stood around the baby so the parents could not see what was happening. They laid the baby on a table. One of the men held a pillow over the baby's face. There was no sound in the room except the muffled crying of the baby's parents. In a few minutes it was over, and the baby's body was wrapped in a white tablecloth. By the next morning the baby's body was gone. I don't know what was done with it, and nobody talked about it again.

I sat in the hiding place for a few days until the morning of the 23rd of April. That morning the neighbor's son, the policeman who warned us about the Aktion, came into our hiding place. He told us that anyone who belonged to the Werterfassung should go to Neska Street for an assembly. He said that the Germans were going to make a new ghetto for the members of the Werterfassung.

As I was leaving the hiding place Mrs. Brozostek handed me a pack of dried bread. I thanked her and we wished each other good-bye.

The leader of the Werterfassung was a SS man named Konrad. He gave out an announcement about the new ghetto for the workers. Members of the Werterfassung and some other work details were offered identification cards that would allow them to remain in the ghetto.

A group of people left the hiding place. Alla and I were among them. As I left the building I could see smoke rising all over the ghetto. To fight the uprising and to get people out of their hiding places the SS had started to set fire to the buildings. Also they would pump poison gas into the basements and into the sewers. Later in concentration camp I met some of the people who had been exposed to the gas. They could talk only in whispers since the gas affected their throats.

We went to Neska Street. Over 1600 Jews assembled there. We got into rows as Konrad stood in front of us. We were told that we were going to the assembly place next to the Jewish Gemeinde. There they were going to organize a new section of the ghetto. With Konrad in front of us we marched up Neska Street. When we got to Zamenhof Street, Konrad turned right and the whole column turned with him. I knew something was wrong because the Gemeinde was to the left, but I continued walking with everybody else. I didn't want to leave the column.

At the end of the street stood a large pair of doors, as wide as the street itself. The doors were swung open to the outside of the ghetto, and we were marched through them.

As soon as we were outside, we were surrounded by armed soldiers, many with dogs. Nobody was able to get away. We were pushed and shoved and hurried to the Umschlagplatz where the train tracks were. By the hundreds we were loaded into freight cars. We were packed in so tight that people had to climb over each other to fit in. Alla was with me in the same car. Then the doors were shut, and the train started moving.

On April 23, 1943 I left Warsaw. Less than six months before I had arrived by train traveling like a human being. I left it packed like an animal.

7
MAJDANEK

I found myself next to a window. It was the best place to be in that freight car. The rest of the car was dark, even during the day, and pitch black during the night. Sometimes there were fights over places near the window.

Most of us stood the whole way. We were packed in so tight that you could remain standing even if you fell asleep. A few people fainted or dropped from exhaustion. But the floor was a dangerous place, and most of those that fell down never got up again.

After traveling for a short while one of the young men among us said that he was with the partisans. He moved over to a small opening in the corner of the freight car and looked out of it. He said that as we left Warsaw we should watch which way the train turned.

"If the train turns onto the track to Treblinka we'll wait till night, break out of the cars, and make a run for it," he said. "Because we'll be going to certain death anyway. Should the train turn onto the track to Lublin it will mean we're going to a camp. Then everyone should remain in the cars."

We all stayed quiet in the car waiting for the word on where we were going. After a few hours, after it was already night, the young man announced we were on the tracks to Lublin.

The train stopped and started many times. We were given no food or drink during the trip. The pack of dried bread I had with me I shared, but it did not last long. We were never allowed out to relieve ourselves. The stench in the car soon became unbearable.

During the stops people in the cars would beg for food or water. They would hold out rings to passersby trying to exchange them for a few drops of water. Some Poles did run over with bottles of water in exchange for the rings.

Normally the trip to Lublin took no more than a few hours. This trip took over two days. We were packed in that rail car the whole time. Finally we arrived at our destination and the doors were opened. The SS guards shouted, "Alles heraus," which meant everybody out. We were hurried out of the cars and into some nearby wooden barracks.

For a whole week the trains from Warsaw would come. Each train would unload thousands of people from the ghetto. You could always tell who was from Warsaw just by looking at them. The people from there were always very pale.

As we were being unloaded out of the cars in Lublin, we were helped by young men who were Polish army prisoners of war. They told us that families would be sent to the work camps at Povnatov and Trebniky and that we should get together, men and women, and sign up as married couples. Anyone who remained as a single person would be sent out of the camp and to a certain death.

A couple of young men suggested that I go with them and register as husband and wife. But I said, "No," to all of them. I didn't want to register as anyone's wife. I was already married and certain that my husband was still alive. Also, since my daughter wasn't with me anymore I didn't really care if I lived or died.

A man I knew named Abraham who, before he came to Lublin, lived in the same house as I did in Warsaw. He was one of the men who got out of the ghetto and into a work camp near Warsaw. A few weeks before we arrived his whole camp was brought to Lublin. He wanted to help me stay in the camp. He was going to bribe some of the officials to let me remain there. I didn't let him. I didn't want to save myself that way. The only hope I still had in the world was that Alter was still alive. Taking up with another man meant the end of that hope.

After a week we were ordered out of the barracks. Alla also did not register as anyone's wife, and together we walked out of the camp. As I walked through the gate I took off the kerchief my father had given me when I left home. I threw it into a ditch by the side of the road. I said better a Pole should find it than a German take it away from me.

SS soldiers guarded us as we walked out of the camp and along a road. A young woman walking near me turned to a German who was guarding us and said, "Soon you'll be making us into soap."

The guard got very angry and shouted at her to shut up. He told her if she said that again he would pull her out of the line and shoot her right there. He said we were not going to die but were going to an Arbeitslager. Arbitslager, in German, meant work camp.

This was on a field near Lublin. We walked there for how long I don't remember. We passed fields surrounded by fences topped with barbed wire. There were men working in these fields. One of the men called out to us and told us we were going to a camp called Majdanek.

Many of us were certain that we were going to die. Some of the people had poison with them and used it. The poison was called sancalya. In English, cyanide, I think. Some even gave it to their children. Also people started throwing away their valuables and tearing up their money. Most of the paper money the people carried was American dollars.

I remember the people in Warsaw always trying to exchange any currency they had for dollars or gold. Everyone was always looking for a way out of the country, and dollars were the best thing to travel with. They considered most other paper currency worthless. I remember walking along that road to Majdanek through ankle deep piles of torn dollars.

This upset the Germans greatly. Not the poisoning, I'm sure, but the torn dollars. They brought a woman, who was also from Warsaw, to talk to us. I did not know her, but many of the others did. She had her child with her. She told us that we were not going to die but were going to work. There were even special places for mothers with children and extra food for them. I remember her saying, "All the children will get rolls and milk."

She said it over and over again, "Rolls and milk." This calmed the people down, and they continued to walk to Majdanek.

Before we got to the camp the older people were separated from us and led away. I saw my neighbor from Warsaw, Mrs. Bshostek, and her six children. The Germans sent Mrs. Bshostek and two of her younger children, her 10 and 12-year old daughters, off with the other old people. As they were being led away the oldest daughter and one of her sons left our group and ran after them. We all cried as we watched them walk off huddled together to what we were sure were to be their deaths.

On the way to Majdanek stood a building called the Sauna. It stood by itself. No other building stood around it, only fields. The Sauna looked different from the other buildings around Lublin. It was surrounded by a fence, topped with barbed wire. At the door to the building stood a big box. It was about 4 feet wide and 6 feet long, and it was full of jewelry and other valuables.

We were told that we would have to give up all of our possessions and clothes but that we could keep our shoes. In the building when we were ordered to take off all our clothes Alla pulled out a bag full of gold pieces. She showed it to me and said, "Mala, what do you think I should do with this?"

I couldn't believe my eyes. I said, "Alla where did you get this?"

She said, "Mala, you're from the provinces. You trust everybody. Why did you think I went dressed the way I did? I had this bag of gold on me the whole time in Warsaw. The way I looked I figured nobody would check if I had any money."

She told me of her father who was a rich jeweler in Warsaw before the war. Before he was taken away he gave a bag of gold to his wife and to all of his children. She didn't want the Germans to get it so she asked me what I thought she should do with it.

I had her divide the gold into 4 piles and put them into the tips of our shoes. I thought since they were going to let us keep our shoes we might still save some of the gold.

Inside the building they took away our clothes and told us to take off our shoes. Then they sent a few hundred women at a time into a chamber. This chamber they said was the showers. It was dark inside. After a while I could see a little better because of a little light that came from some painted over windows. The walls and floor of the chamber were made of smooth gray concrete. There were concrete benches along side the walls. High up on the walls, against the ceiling, were the small windows that were closed. In the chamber, someone said, they could send in gas or water, whichever they wanted. I was sure this was my end and that I was in the gas chamber. But to my surprise only water came out of the showerheads.

In the early 1970s I was called to testify at the German consulate in New York. The Commandant and some Ukrainian guards from Majdanek had been caught and were being brought to trial. During questioning the German Consul asked me, "Were you ever in the crematorium?"

I answered, "I think if I had been in a crematorium I would not be here today."

The Consul asked me to describe how I came to Majdanek. I told him of the walk from Lublin and coming to the Sauna. He asked me to describe the Sauna inside and out, which I did. After I was done he said, "You were in a crematorium. That building in the field was Majdanek's crematorium."

Until then I did not know for sure that the chamber I was in was indeed a gas chamber.

When we came out of the showers we saw that our clothes were taken away but our shoes remained where we had left them. We were shown a pile of clean clothes, rags really, and told to get quickly dressed. All the woman had to wear dresses. Everyone had only one dress. We didn't have time to even straighten our clothes. Some of us didn't have enough time to even get fully dressed as we were chased out of the building. We just barely got our own shoes back as everyone was hurried into the camp at Majdanek.

In the camp we were given numbers that were to be sewn onto our clothes. 25 lashes was the punishment if the number fell off.

We were assigned to a barracks. The barracks were wooden buildings called blocks. Each block had a few hundred women in it. We were on the 4th or 5th field in Majdanek, I don't remember which. The camp was divided into 5 fields. One field was for the women and the rest for the men.

I remember some men coming over to the fence between the fields and asking us where we were from. Majdanek was near Lublin, and there were women from around Lublin among us. People were always trying to find, or learn the fate of, someone they knew.

I remember the food there as being better than in the other camps. I remember the soup that was given out once a day. The soup usually had a piece of sausage or potato in it. If you were among the first to get the soup there was enough to fill you up. We were each allowed only one bowl, never more. If you were among the people who worked far away from where the soup was given out, sometimes you didn't get any. Also because of Alla's gold, we were able to buy extra food on the camp's black market, so in Majdanek I did not go hungry.

At first I worked in the camp vegetable garden. The SS that watched over us were very mean. One of the Germans was named Brigita. For no reason at all she would start beating one of us. The beatings were 50 lashes on our bare backs. Many people ended up in the hospital after a beating.

We sometimes came into contact with some Poles who lived nearby and worked in the camp. We were able to trade with them for extra food as long as the Germans didn't find out. If the Germans found anything of value on us it was taken away. There was a rule against having any money or gold. If anyone was found with them they were beaten right away, sometimes even executed.

Once Alla gave me a 5 or 10 ruble gold piece. It was a gold piece from Russia from before the revolution. It had the Czar's image on one side and on the other it said 5 or 10 rubles. But we figured value in dollars, and these gold pieces were very valuable. They were 22k gold, which was more gold than other gold pieces the same size. I traded it for some long breads and some eggs. I had to do it, but the whole time I remember thinking how dangerous it was.

One time I was working on a building detail. I was wearing a sweater with two breast pockets. In one pocket I had a gold piece. In my hands I was carrying 3 or 4 bricks. Brigita came over to me and put her hand in the pocket that had nothing in it. She didn't find anything, but still she hit me in the face with her fist. She hit me so hard that my nose started bleeding. If she had found the gold piece in the other pocket she certainly would have beaten me more or even killed me. Any black market trading was severely punished.

Shindala Lacher, who I knew in Warsaw as a friend of Sala's, became my close friend in Majdanek. Many years after the war, she testified against Brigita in a war crimes trial.

Later, I was lucky to get work on a detail that was digging ditches for the sewers that ran between the barracks. I volunteered for this work because it put me near where the food was given out. The people who had to come far for food, would often get very little, or none at all. The people who got there last would fight over the soup and often spill the last of it. Watching it I would laugh and cry at the same time, seeing people act like animals. But hunger made them act this way.

After a few days in Majdanek, Alla found some old school friends from Warsaw, from before the war. I didn't like her friends and thought they were just using her for her money. After awhile Alla spent most of her time with her friends.

Once when I was standing in line for food Alla handed me a small pack of gold. She said she was going to get washed and would get it back when she returned. One of the Polish prisoners, who was dishing out the soup, saw her hand me something. Her name was Zosia. When I got to the soup Zosia told me to stand aside and wait for her.

After the soup was all given out she told me to follow her into the barracks. There she told me to give her what Alla gave me.. I pretended to not know what she was talking about. She said, "If you don't give it to me I'll call over one of the SS guards, and he'll check to see what you have on you."

I had no choice so I gave the pack of gold to her.

When Alla returned I told her she hadn't been careful enough when she gave me the gold. I told her what had happened between Zosia and me. Alla told me to come with her. Together we approached Zosia. Alla told her to give it back or she would tell the SS about the gold. It was also against the rules for the Polish prisoners to have any gold. The two of them came to an agreement and decided to split the pack of gold.

I did not spend much time with Alla after that.

Two weeks after I came to Majdanek Sala And Genia came there too. They had lived through the worst of the uprising and had a lot to tell. I was happy to see them. Yagha Gold had come to Lublin with them. From Lublin she tried to run away but was shot and killed.

In Majdanek I also found a good friend of mine from Warsaw. We both lived at Muranowska 38 and worked together in the Werterfassung. Her name was Rutta Bucksner.

I will never forget her. She was young and pretty with dark hair. Her husband was just grabbed on a street in the ghetto and taken out. Rutta never knew where he was taken or what happened to him.

Rutta had a six-year old daughter that lived with her in Warsaw. A neighbor watched her daughter while we were at work.

She was always very afraid. She was envious of me that I didn't have my child with me anymore. Once, in Warsaw, I said to her, "Rutta, I'm sure you and your daughter will survive the war."

She looked at me and said, "I don't feel that we will. I feel that I will die with my child."

"Rutta don't talk like that," I said.

She and her daughter came to Lublin at the same time that I did. We didn't see each other there. In Lublin the Germans asked people about any skills they had. They were looking for people who knew how to make brushes. In Warsaw one of the big factories made brushes. Rutta said that she knew how and she was sent away to work. Her daughter was separated from her and sent to Majdanek. A few days after we got to Majdanek a friend saw Rutta's daughter at the barracks where the children were.

Two weeks later Rutta also came to Majdanek. She told us that the Germans tested the people to see if they really knew how to make brushes, and she had failed. So they sent her to Majdanek.

She could have gone and lived with her daughter. Instead she chose to live in the barracks in which I was living. Every morning she would go and see her daughter. She would help her get dressed and washed. Then she would go to work with the women of our barracks. When she could she would bring her daughter some extra food. Rutta would visit her every day, but she was afraid to live with her.

A few weeks later, early in the morning, Rutta went to see her child. Suddenly the SS surrounded the barracks where the mothers and children were living. Rutta was caught in the barracks with her daughter. The SS took them all away to the gas chambers. The thing that Rutta felt would happen, happened.

I didn't stay long in Majdanek. But I still saw many tragedies. The women were beaten and killed. One girl I saw hanged. She had been caught trying to escape. Before she was hung the Lagerfearer asked her, loud enough for all of us to hear, if she was sorry she tried to escape. She screamed out, "No. Because in this camp there is only death and to try to escape is to choose life."

The Lagerfearer quickly put the rope around her neck and she was hung. Her body was left hanging for 24 hours as a warning to the rest of us.

Every Sunday morning there was a selekcja. A selekcja is what we called the selections. Those who failed the selekcja were later taken to the gas chambers because they were not fit enough to work. For the Germans if you were not fit enough to work you were not fit enough to live.

One of the reasons for failing a selekcja was to have blisters on your feet. A lot of the girls were taken to the gas chambers because they had blisters. Most of these people had been in the Warsaw ghetto for a long time. There they had very little sun and became very pale. Their feet blistered easily when they started spending so much time in the sun.

Once a young girl came over to me and asked to borrow my boots. She had blisters on her feet. She said to me, "You have very healthy feet. Please lend me your boots till after the selekcja."

The boots were high enough to cover up her blisters so they would not be seen during the selekcja. When the Germans were taking the Jews out of my town, my father told all of his children to go and have a good pair of shoes made for themselves. He knew that if we were going to go to a work camp we would need a good pair of shoes. I got a pair of boots that laced up the front. That pair of boots I lent to the young girl. After the selekcja she returned the boots to me.

I also met a girl who was caught hiding in Germany with a Polish pass. She was caught because she never wrote or received any letters. This made the people she was staying with suspicious.

I stayed in Majdanek for about 10 weeks, until the middle of July. At that time people were saying that the Germans were going to take us to another Arbeitslager in Germany. We knew that they were going to take only the healthiest among us. Everyone wanted to be selected for the work camp.

I wanted to leave because of Alla. She spent all of her time with her other friends. At times she treated me with obvious charity, and I didn't like it. Once she walked by me with her friends and threw me a piece of bread. They all laughed.

The first time I went through the selection for the work camp I was not chosen. You would know if you were picked when the doctor indicated to the scribe standing next to him to write down your number. Our numbers were on our clothes.

I ran around the building and tried to make myself look better. I pinched my cheeks to make them redder. Some of the other women used a reddish stain, from paper that was used to darken coffee, to redden their cheeks. Then I got back into line and again went through the selection. The second time I was picked.

Before I left Majdanek, Alla came over to say good-bye. I saw her again during the war in Auschwitz. She came to Auschwitz a few weeks after I did but got sick with malaria after a few days. The Germans sent her and a number of other malaria patients back to Majdanek, but I didn't know this. As soon as I heard she was taken away I thought her dead. I saw her one more time, after the war in Warsaw. I will tell more about that later.

I thought myself very lucky to be leaving Majdanek. The Germans gathered us together and marched us to the train tracks. We were loaded into freight cars.

When I was brought to Majdanek we were packed into the cars so tightly that one would not have fallen down even if they had fallen asleep. Then we were over 100 people to a car. In comparison to that trip, on this one we traveled in style. We were only 45 to 50 people in each freight car. Our car was all women. On top of each car sat an SS soldier with a gun.

After traveling awhile, word spread among us that our destination was Auschwitz. When I heard the word Auschwitz a lump formed in my throat. I remembered hearing the name Auschwitz when I was still at home. It was where the Germans sent the officers of the Polish army. Those that returned home came back as ashes.

8

BIRKENAU, AUSCHWITZ

When I arrived in Auschwitz I did not have to go through a selection. Our trainload of people came as workers. We were led into the Sauna and showered. Then some woman cut off our hair. We looked at each other, at first, not knowing who the other person was. We looked so different. Then they tattooed a number and a triangle on my arm. The number was 46981.

My arm swelled up around the tattoo. That happened to a lot of us. It was very painful, but in a few days the swelling went down, and the pain stopped.

First our group was sent to Lager A. We were there for only a short while. Lager A was the quarantine section. It also included the hospital. The hospital was called the Rewier. Lager B was still being built. When it was done we were sent there. Lager B was the Arbeitslager, the work camp. All the working Kommandos were housed in Lager B.

Each lager consisted of many barracks. The barracks were called blocks. The head of each barracks was called the Blockalteste, which meant block leader. In Auschwitz the Blockaltestes were Jews from Slovakia. They were the first Jews that were sent to Auschwitz. They were the labor that built the camp. Very few of them survived. From among those that did survive the German picked the barracks' leaders and their helpers. Also they were the workers in the camp offices.

Each of the barracks housed between 600 and 700 women. The barracks were divided into 8 to 12 sections. Each section was called a sthouba. Each sthouba had a woman assigned to it called a Sthoubova, which meant section leader. One of the Sthoubova's jobs was to go with their Blockalteste to the kitchen and the bread counter, bring the food for the barracks and give it out. Also their job was to wake us up for work each morning, and to make sure everything in her section was clean and in order. Our first Sthoubova was named Susan. Each barracks also had 2 to 4 girls called Wachters. They were the night watch. They made sure nothing was stolen during the night. Each Blockalteste also had a secretary to help her out. The secretary was called the Blockschreiber. So each barrack had a leader, a secretary, 8 to 12 Sthoubovakas and 2 to 4 Wachters. Most of these were the women who had been in Auschwitz the longest.

We slept on wooden planks. At first they were bare, but later we were able to add straw. The planks were in three tiers that ran the length of the barracks. They were separated every few feet by wooden posts. The space between the posts was called a coya. In a coya slept 6 to 8 woman.

Two rows of coyas ran along the walls, and a third one down ran the middle. The row against one of the walls was divided to make room for the door to the barracks. In front of the door was a space for giving out the food. Next to that was a small room for the Blockalteste. There were windows on each side of the door, halfway between the door and the end of the barracks.

We were in the part of the Auschwitz complex that was called Birkenau. My lager and my work were in Birkenau. At the beginning I picked leaves, called pokrziwa in Polish. In German they were called brenesel. They burned the skin when we picked them. They were added to the soup that was cooked in the camp. The plants grew on the bottom of ponds that were really just flooded meadows. Sometimes after a big rain the water was up to our necks when we reached down to pick the leaves.

My first work group was called the 105th Kommando. We were about 150 women divided into three groups of 50. Each group had a Vorarbeiter, or Kapo. They were our work leaders. Many of the Kapos were criminals. They were known by the black triangles on their clothing. Ours was a German prostitute. She was in charge of our work details. A lot of the Kapos were street women from Germany.

Each Kapo had one or two Jewish helpers, and over each Kapo was an SS man. When we were working the SS man usually stayed in a hut nearby. We were watched over by the Kapos and their helpers.

Once a group of SS men came to our kommando to watch us work. They were very important SS. Their uniforms were black. The camp SS wore gray or green uniforms.

One of them started yelling at our Kapo. He said that she was no better then the rest of us. He then pushed her into the water, told her to work with us, and not to just watch us.

I noticed something about Birkenau early on. Birkenau was a place where people just disappeared. Many friends disappeared, and when they were gone nobody spoke about them anymore.

I remember seeing a group of young men marching to work every day. They were beautiful young men. They were Russian officers, and they marched with such grace and dignity. Everyone stopped to watch as they went by, but then one day they too just disappeared.

A friend of mine from Majdanek came to me in the first few days we were in Birkenau, and told me she was pregnant. She had heard that pregnant woman could get extra food if they registered. She asked me to come with her and pretend to be pregnant, but I told her I didn't trust the Germans. I was sure it was a trick. She went by herself, and within a few days she disappeared.

After about two months in Birkenau I was sent to the 103rd Kommando. This was called Kommando Strasenboun. There were 500 women in this kommando. Strasenboun meant road builders. All 500 women from Kommando Strasenboun were issued uniforms taken from captured Russian soldiers.

Everyone also had to wear something on their head, a hat or a kerchief. This was a rule for everyone in the camp. You had to have your head covered all the time.

There was a lot of building going on around the camp, especially along the rail line.

For the next 15 months our kommando worked there in Birkneau building a whole city for the SS. We cleared the fields, and built roads, parks and buildings. The buildings were used as hospitals for the wounded from the Russian front. Also we built a crematorium for the Germans that died in their hospital.

Thousands of us died on that kommando.

We were 500 women and 2000 men working on the roads and buildings. Among the men we worked with were Volksdeutsch. They were the machinists and engineers that oversaw our work. It was with these Germans that we traded.

I started trading after I found the 46 dollars in a skirt. We 500 women were divided into 10 groups of 50. The 10 groups were assigned to different tasks. As one group carried stones another would carry kise. Kise was a mixture of sand and small stones.

Whenever we had something to trade we would signal to the Volksdeutschen. They had a small building where they would eat their lunch and store their tools. That's where we had to bring the items to trade and get paid for them. Usually we did this in a group of three women. The Kapos would often leave us in the care of their helpers. A few of the helpers were no better than the Kapos, but most of them would help us if they could. Most of the Kapo's helpers were Jewish girls, and they would help by watching for the Kapos and the SS. The Volksdeutschen would watch out too, and when it was clear we would sneak over and do our trading.

If we were with the group carrying the kise going in one direction we would walk past the group carrying stones walking in the opposite direction. If it was clear, the three of us would quickly join the other group going the other way. In this way we maneuvered our way to the building the Volksdeutschen were in. Sometimes it would take an hour of walking back and forth to get there.

Salla taught me how to deal with these Germans. Before I found the money in the skirt, she had had a gold coin, worth about 20 dollars, that she had sold to them. Salla had borrowed the coin from Shindala.

After I found the money Shindala got to work in the Blue Affect. The Blue Affect was the place where the items that were taken away from the people who were sent into the gas chambers were brought. There the items were packed up and sent to Germany. Shindala and the others who worked there would sneak out small items. The girls who worked on the Ausser Kommandos, the outside kommandos, would take these items and trade them for items we could not get in the camp.

Sometimes a Volksdeutsch would ask us to bring out certain items. Once they asked for silk kerchiefs. I told Shindala to look for them. She brought me some, and I sold them to the Germans. We then divided whatever I got for those kerchiefs.

If we could not get what we wanted from the Blue Affect we would go to the women who worked in the Canada. The Canada was the place right near the crematoriums. They would get things before they were sent to the Blue Affect.

Once on the way back to the camp, word got around that we were going to be searched at the entrance. Everybody started to remove any contraband that they were hiding. The whole road back to camp was littered with valuables. Hundreds of cigarettes and pieces of food were thrown away. There were eggs and bread and scarves all over the ground. Anything one could want one could just pick up, but nobody did because anyone caught with them was severely beaten. For many, a year's worth of dealing had to be thrown away.

Lots of our trading also took place in the toilets. Mostly food was traded there. One young girl from Greece, named Stella, became my friend there. She was 16 or 17 years old, and terribly thin. Whenever she had sausage she would trade it for a piece of bread. If by the end of the day I had any food left I sometimes gave it to her. If she still had her sausage I'd tell her to eat it too.

I tried not to take any food back to the barracks with me. If I didn't eat it I tried to trade it for cigarettes or money. Cigarettes or money I could carry in my pockets or in a rag and take to work with me. Food was too big and had to be hidden in the barracks, but any food hidden there was usually stolen during the day. Lots of fights broke out when we returned from work and someone found their food gone.

A short time after I found the money, Alla came to Auschwitz. She had no more gold and couldn't get any extra food. Her old friends abandoned her as soon as the gold was gone. I lent her some money to help her start trading. I did owe her for her earlier kindness, and I didn't hold a grudge. I realized that my anger was what got me into Auschwitz to begin with.

After 3 or 4 weeks Alla got sick and was taken to the Rewier. I didn't see her again in Auschwitz and thought she was taken away after a selection.

In Birkenau our days started at 3 o'clock in the morning. Those that wanted to could run and get washed. Tea, or sometimes soup, was then given out. We each had our own metal dish and spoon. We always had to carry them with us. By 4 A.M. we had to be out of our barracks and assembled on the Appel.

The Appel was the roll call, which was held in front of our barracks. There were 60,000 women in Auschwitz, and we had to be counted twice a day. If the count wasn't right, or if someone was missed, they started all over again. We would stand there for hours as we were counted.

On the Appel everyone was assigned to a row with 9 others. The same ten had to stand together every day. This way if someone was missing they knew right away who it was. After our barracks was counted we didn't have to stand in rows anymore, but the same ten had to stay near each other until we were ordered back into our rows and marched to work. But until then, especially when it turned cold, we would stand huddled together for warmth.

On many days there was a fog in the morning since Auschwitz was in a valley near a river. We would be kept standing on the Appel until the fog lifted for fear that one of us would run away, especially the ones in the Ausser Kommandos. Sometimes we waited till 10 o'clock.

On nice days we would go out by the time it started getting light. We got to our work area as soon as it was light enough to work. This way the Germans did not miss out on a minute of the time we could be working.

Until the end of 1943 our Kommando was not allowed to wear shoes, or anything on our feet, to work. At the end of November we were given wooden clogs, but they offered no protection from the rain and cold. If one had some rags they could wrap them around their feet. But even with rags, by December, it was so cold that our feet froze as we waited on the Appel.

To fight the cold we had to keep shifting feet. As I stood on one foot I rubbed the other foot on my leg for warmth. When the foot I was standing on couldn't take it anymore I would switch feet and rub that one to warm it up. This went on for hours till we finally got to go to work.

Every day I would scan the sky for evidence that spring was coming. My feet were the first to feel the days getting warmer.

When we were finally marched off to work our Blockelteste, or her secretary, would lead us to the camp gate. There we were turned over to SS guards with dogs. They in turn would lead us to our work.

Even on rainy days we worked: no matter how hard it rained. We worked in the mud and got soaked to the skin. When we returned to our camp we would stand on the Appel in the pouring rain till we were all counted. We would return dripping wet to our barracks. We took off our wet things, hung them up, and got into our bunks to sleep. By 3 o'clock in the morning, when we were awakened, our clothes were still wet. We had to put them on and go out into the night air. Again we stood for hours on the Appel. This was how many of us got sick, and this was how many of us died.

In Birkenau I got sick from typhus. A lot of us got sick from typhus and from dysentery. With dysentery everything that you ate went right through you.

When I got sick with typhus many others in the camp were sick with it too. There was a big epidemic of typhus at the time. At our barracks we laid around like fallen logs. The Rewier was full of people. Just feeling sick couldn't get you into the Rewier. You had to have a high fever at least. Outside the Rewier the dead were stacked like firewood.

I was so sick that I saw wheels turning before my eyes. I could not stand most of the time. But no matter how sick I was, I was more afraid to go to the Rewier. There I was sure they would send me straight to the gas chamber.

I was so sick that I remember hoping I would just die. At times we were jealous of the people who died naturally, but we were very afraid of being sent to the gas chamber. I don't know why, but even when I hoped I would die, I was afraid of going to the gas chamber. A lot of the girls died in our barracks. Some took their lives by grabbing the wire at the edge of the camp, but it was the ones that died in their sleep that we envied. I hoped that if I had to go to the Rewier I would be lucky enough to just die peacefully as I lay my head down to sleep.

The day after I got sick the Blockalteste and her secretary took 25 to 30 of us over to the Rewier. At the Rewier we were turned away because they were too full and had no place to put us. Our Blockalteste was told to take us to Block 25 of Lager A.

Nobody ever returned from Lager A's Block 25. The only people who left Block 25 were taken right to the crematoriums. Walking to Block 25 I fell down. I didn't fall down from being ill but from fear. Here I felt I was looking death in the face, and I was afraid.

For the longest time in camp I acted the hero. Whenever others would despair I would talk them into having hope. I would always tell others not to be afraid, but on the way to Block 25 I lost all my nerve. Some of the other girls, who were as sick as I was, helped me get to my feet and continue walking.

As we neared Block 25 the secretary from our barracks came running and calling the name of our Blockalteste. The secretary's name was Etichka. I can't remember her last name, but I do remember her as a very good person. Many times she saved my life. Our Blockalteste's name was Etta Locks.

When we heard Etichka calling we all stopped and turned around. She came up to us and said to the Blockalteste, "Etta turn around with them. I talked the people at the Rewier into letting our girls in. They will put them two or three in a bed if they have to. Only don't take them to Block 25."

We turned around and were led back to the Rewier. There they let us in. The Rewier looked like any other barracks. There was no medicine there, but the food was a little better. If anyone got better it was mostly from the rest they got there.

I stayed in the Rewier for a week. I couldn't keep down the food they gave me, and of course we got no medication, but still most of the girls in our group got better. I had some money left over so I had Salla buy me some fruit.

The first few days in the Rewier there was a very sick young woman in the bed next to me. She wasn't Jewish and had one of the older numbers on her arm. I think she was a political prisoner. They took away our clothes so you couldn't tell what kind of prisoner one was unless you asked.

Once when she spoke to me I had to lean very close to hear her, but I didn't understand her language. She motioned to me, and to the girl in the bed on the other side of her, to help her sit up. We got her up, but she didn't have the strength to stay up, and soon fell back down on her back.

The woman knew she was going to die soon. She showed us a package she received from home. She kept it under her head like a pillow so no one would steal it. The non-Jewish inmates were allowed to receive such packages. She motioned for me, and her other neighbor, to take the package when she was dead. We sat there staring at her, I'm ashamed to say, waiting for her to die. We wanted that package.

A few hours later she stopped breathing. I took the package from behind her head and was going to share it with the other girl. As soon as I opened the box the other girls in the room descended on me like locust. Hands started grabbing for the box. As it was being ripped from my hands I reached in and grabbed the first thing I could. It was a large sweet onion. Over the next two days I ate that onion. I'm not sure, but I think eating that onion helped me get over the typhus. Over those two days I first started feeling better.

After about a week I was ordered to leave the Rewier. The nurses said that I was fit enough to return to work. Everyone leaving the Rewier had to go through a selection. I was sure that I wasn't well enough to pass a selection. I would not leave. Whenever someone said it was time I left I would begin to cry. The nurses would say to each other that I was lazy and didn't want to return to work. But the real reason I didn't want to leave was because I feared being sent to the gas chamber.

A day or two later all 25 or 30 of us were signed out of the hospital at the same time. We were sent to the Sauna.

The Sauna was a big brick building. It had only one floor with lots of rooms and lots of corridors. The windows were covered with iron bars. This was the building where they made the selection for work or the gas chamber.

We walked into a room that had benches along the wall. The benches were like in a stadium that went higher one row behind the other. The benches took up half the room. The walls were brick, and there were no windows in this room.

We were ordered to undress and sit on the benches. We sat there naked, until told to line up, and be examined by a doctor and a group of SS. With the SS was our Blockelteste and her secretary.

As the doctor was about to examine us, in walked the head of the camp. His name was Commandant Hoss. We called him Hessler. With him was a woman named Mala Zimetbaum.

Mala Zimetbaum, God rest her soul, was known to all of us. Everyone looked up to her, even the Germans. She was a Polish Jew, born in Krakow and grew up in Belgium. It was said that she spoke six languages and was very educated. Because she was so educated the Germans used her as an interpreter. She was taken around to all the offices. I read, after the war, that there was a plaque in her honor on the street where her family home was in Belgium.

Mala was allowed to have her hair. We had to have ours cut every so often so it didn't get too long. She also was dressed better then we were.

She said to the camp commandant, "I can't get any work done because I don't have enough workers. These look like healthy women. They came from Kommando 103. You must send them back to Kommando 103."

The camp commandant looked at us and said, "Are you girls healthy enough to go back to work?"

As if in one voice we said, "Jawohl!"

We said it so loud that some of us almost fell over. I was so weak at the time that if a hair was out of place I would have fallen over.

The commandant stopped the selection and told us all to go back to work. That day Mala Zimetbaum saved my life.

Mala Zimetbaum died for Kiddush Hashem (martyrdom for the glorification and sanctification of God).

Going to work one day, this was in the spring of 1944, we heard that Mala escaped from Auschwitz. It was said that an SS man helped her and her Polish lover escape. Both of them were dressed up in SS uniforms and sneaked out of the camp. We were very thrilled with her escape.

A few days later we heard that Mala was caught. At first I didn't believe it. I said that if the Germans had her they would show her to us. I told the others that the Germans were telling us this because they didn't want us to try and escape too.

The next day, as we returned to the camp from work, Mala was standing on a platform at the entrance to the camp, near the Sauna. The Germans had cut off all of her hair. She once had beautiful hair.

As we filed back into the camp we were ordered to line up in the square. They brought Mala to us. We could see that they were going to make an example of her. An SS man standing in front of Mala started talking to us. He said that we were here to work, and that the Germans had no intention of harming us.

As he was talking Mala gave out a yell and fell to the ground. Someone had given her a blade, and she had cut one of her wrists with it. The German leaned over her and said, "You dumb ass. Why did you do that?"

The German tried to stop the bleeding by grabbing her wrist. With her other hand Mala slapped the German in the face. She hit him so hard that I thought his head would come off.

The German started shouting at some of the girls in the front row. He told them to put Mala on a cart and take her to the crematoriums. An SS guard with a dog watched the girls as they pushed the cart towards the crematoriums.

Later that evening one of the girls who went along with the cart told us what had happened along the way. Mala told them why she had escaped. She said that she knew that she could have survived the war. That the Germans respected her. But she could not take it anymore. She could not stand idly by as the Germans killed the Jews by the hundreds of thousands.

She had seen the gassing of women and children. She wanted to get out and tell the world what was happening here. She didn't know if the world knew that the Germans were killing all the Jews. She tried to get to a radio station and broadcast a message to the world.

The German walking with them told her to be quiet. She turned to him and said, "Soon I'll be quiet, but the ones that live will not be quiet. They will tell the world what you Germans did here in Auschwitz."

Mala died on the way to the crematorium. The young men who worked there, the Sonderkommandos, were told of her coming. They prepared her, with honors, for the crematorium. The girls stood there crying as they burned her body. Mala's Polish lover, who was also caught, was hung in the men's camp.

9
THE BLEEDING SKY

The week I lay in the Rewier, sick with typhus, I learned that my two younger sisters were also in Auschwitz. For months both Yenta and Sara were near me in Birkenau, and I did not know about it.

As I lay in the hospital a woman in a bed near me looked over and asked, "Where do I know you from? Your face looks so familiar."

I started naming places. Warsaw. Majdanek. I didn't think to name my hometown. "No," she said. She had never been to any of those places.

I did not recognize her, but I asked her where she had come from. She said she came from a camp in Inowroclaw. I said, "My two sisters are in that camp."

She asked me their names and I said, "Yenta and Sara Liss."

Her eyes widened and she said, "That's why you look so familiar. You and your sisters look so alike. But don't you know, they are here in Birkenau for 3 or 4 months already? We came together from Inowroclaw."

I, of course, didn't know that. As soon as she told me my sisters were there I jumped out of bed, but I was too weak to go very far, and the nurses made me lay back down.

This woman was from a town near my home called Wieruszow. At the same time as the Germans were rounding up Jews from our town they were also rounding them up in

Wieruszow. She was sent to Inowroclaw at the same time as my sisters.

She got better a few days before I did and was released from the hospital. She told my sisters about me. That same day Yenta and a cousin of ours, Fedgda Rissel, came to see me. Fedgda Rissel was our first cousin. She was my mother's sister's daughter, and she was 5 years younger than me.

We hugged and kissed and cried. They both looked so thin. We told each other our stories. Everyone in the Rewier came to listen and to cry.

They were also in Lager B, but were not yet assigned to a kommando. My youngest sister, Sara, couldn't come to visit me in the Rewier. I was going to see her when I got better, but even when I was released from the hospital I wasn't well enough to go see her. After I was released from the hospital, and saved by Mala Zimetbaum in the Sauna, I was sent to the quarantine barracks.

I was in quarantine for about a week. One day while I was there I went outside and stood along the fence that surrounded the quarantine barracks. The quarantine barracks were next to the barracks where the bread was distributed. I stood looking at the girls lined up for bread, and there I saw my sister Sara.

I hardly recognized her. She had gotten so thin. She looked half as big as she did at home. I called her name, and she ran over. We kissed and held hands through the fence. All the other girls gathered around us as we tried to talk. We hadn't seen each other for over a year and a half. We had a lot to say to each other, but I could not stop crying. Every time she asked about our parents or about Nunyala I just started crying again.

In a short while she had to go. So much happened after that, that we never had a chance to talk much again.

By the time I got better my sister Yenta got sick. She had dysentery. I spent all I had to get her some extra bread. She was supposed to burn the bread to darken it some before eating it. It was said that burnt bread was good for dysentery, but later I learned that she was so hungry that she ate the bread as soon as I left. She could not even wait to burn it some. Every day she got weaker and weaker, and in a few days she died.

Sara lived for a few weeks after Yenta died. She took our sister's death very hard. Yenta was also my sister, and I grieved for her greatly, but Sara was very close to her and never got over her death.

Since they were taken from our home, they had been together. In the camp they were in before Auschwitz, Sara worked as a maid to the wife of the Lagerfearer. The Lagerfearer was the head of the camp. He had five children, and every day he would send Sara to his house to help his wife. His children got very close to Sara. When the Germans ordered all the inmates from the camp sent to Auschwitz the Lagerfearer told her that she wouldn't have to go. That he would hide her in his house so she could stay with his family.

Sara told him that she would stay if he would also hide her sister Yenta there too. But he could not hide two of them. One he could get away with, but if caught hiding two Jews he would have been sent to the Eastern front. The Germans always feared being sent to the Eastern front. So Sara came to Auschwitz rather then be separated from her older sister.

Sara also got sick from dysentery. Again I ran around and got her bread and some soup. I would get up an hour before everyone else and run to the kitchens to get something warm for her. I would hide outside the kitchen and when nobody was looking I would run inside and dip my bowl into a large pot of hot soup. I then ran all the way to my sister's barracks, spilling half the soup along the way, just to bring something warm to my sister.

She got over the dysentery, but right away there was a selection for her barracks and she did not pass it. When I heard she was better I went to see her, but by the time I got to her barracks she had already been taken to the gas chamber.

This was around Christmas time, 1943. For Christmas the Germans gave everyone a whole loaf of bread. When I came into Sara's barracks to see her a friend of hers gave me her bread. Sara asked her to give it to me and to say good-bye.

That's how I lost my two dear younger sisters in Auschwitz.

At the time my sisters and cousin Rissel were taken from our home, thirty other young women from our town were also taken. That was on the 15th of May, 1942. A number of them were in the same barracks as my sisters.

When I was sick in the Rewier I had told my sister Yenta that when I was well enough I'd come over to their barracks and see them all. But by the time I got well there were only a few of them still there. Some were in the Rewier. Most had already died. The only ones still there were Hinda Jusefowitz and Rose Etta Pinkus. Hinda survived the war, and today she lives in Cleveland, Ohio.

Rose Etta Pinkus was one of those girls who had a bad reputation at home, but my sisters told me she was very good to them in the other camp. She worked as a cook in Inowroclaw and was able to steal some extra food. She brought the food back to their barracks and shared it with my sisters and the other girls, never asking payment for any of it.

Rose Etta was one of the few in their barracks who was given a job. She worked in the one of the camp factories called the Weberei.

One day when I came back into my barracks after work, I found Rose Etta standing in middle of the barracks. Her face was black as coal, and she was crying. I asked her what was wrong. She said that she was sent to our barracks as punishment. For doing a poor job in the Weberei she now had to work in the Ausser Kommando.

I told her not to cry. I was doing very well with my dealings and told her I'd take care of her. She had been good to my sisters, and I was going to repay her kindness. I told the Blockaltester to put her near me, and she did. For the rest of the time in Auschwitz I looked after her as if she were my sister. She helped me with my tradings, and I shared my extra food with her. If not for me Rose Etta would have died in Auschwitz.

As it turned out, Rose Etta survived the war but came to a bad end anyway. After the liberation, she was killed in our hometown by the Armja Krajowa, the Polish Home Army.

One of the people who helped Rose Etta and me survive was Wolf Rosenblat. He was the grandson of our town's Shochet (ritual slaughter.) Today Wolf lives in Israel.

Wolf worked in one of the first kommandos that built Auschwitz. We never saw him in the camp, but whenever he could he sent us some food. He would sent it over with a man who worked with us on the Ausser Kommando.

That winter I bribed my way into a job in the Weberei, where Rose Etta had worked. It was not the best indoor kommando, but it was the best I could do since it was already winter. The Weberei was a clothing mill, but our work was to rip rags into strips. We each had a quota of rags to rip and this took all day.

I worked there for 2 or 3 weeks, but it was terrible job. The dust from tearing the rags made it hard to breath. Also since I couldn't do any trading there I could not get anything extra to eat. So, on purpose, I didn't fill my quota, and as punishment I was sent back to the Aussa Kommando.

No Lager was good. No place under the Germans was good, but Birkenau was the worst. Most of my time there I lived in Lager B, Block 27. The back section of Lager B was Blocks 25, 26 and 27. Block 27 was nearest the fence.

In Block 27 I shared a small section, what we called a coya, with 8 or 9 other women. The coya was 3 planks of wood, one on top of the other, that we slept on. The plank I slept on was next to the window. The window was painted over, but I had scratched away a little of the paint in the corner of the window so I could see out. The window looked out on the railroad tracks where the transports came into Birkenau. This section of tracks was called the Rampa. Beyond the tracks I could see some woods. Past the woods I could see the smoke rising from the crematoriums.

Whenever the transports came in a whistle would sound, and we were rushed inside our barracks. This was called a block spree. The transports came into the camp only a few hundred feet from our barracks. Looking out at the transports was not allowed, but I did.

Out of the window I could see the people being unloaded from the trains. I saw them lined up and made to file past some Germans for a selection. I saw one group would be taken in the direction of the crematoriums. It was always the larger group.

By the end of 1943 the crematoriums burned day and night. From my bed I could hear the screams from the gas chamber. It was indescribable. I cannot put it into words.

The air hung heavy with the smoke from the crematoriums. Next to the crematoriums fires were always burning. It was said that they were also burning people in large pits next to the crematoriums. In silhouette I could see people walking in front of the fires. It was a vision of hell.

Toward the evening the sky took on the same color as the fires. Everything took on that color, the sky, the buildings, even the ground. Just before the sunset the red in the sky would deepen to the color of blood. I imagined the sky bleeding. I imagined the heavens suffering with us. To this day a red sunset reminds me of the bleeding sky of Auschwitz.

I would lie in my bunk and cry. I would ask God why we deserved this. Of all the people in the world why was this our lot? Of all the nations why were we being destroyed?

This was Birkenau. By day we went to work from Lager B. It was an Arbeitslager, and everyone had to go out to work. Many times when we returned from work we would be stopped at the entrance to the camp. Waiting for us would be the Blockalteste, her secretary, and some Germans. We would be led to the Sauna for a selection.

In the Sauna we had to get completely undressed. We had to go through a doorway into a room where a German doctor would examine us. Standing next to the doctor was Etichka, the secretary from our block. If you didn't pass the selection he would indicate to the secretary to record your number. Someone whose number was recorded wasn't taken right away. The next day, or the day after that, your number would be called out, and you would be taken away. You would know where you were going. You would know it was the end, but by then most people had already lost the will to live. They would go with a sense of resignation to the lorries that took them to the gas chamber.

At every selection almost half of us would not pass. Each time over 200 women were sent to the gas chamber. Then more women would be added to our kommando bringing us back to 500.

We feared these selections more than anything else. Once, when we came to the Sauna, we saw trucks outside. We had never seen them there before. We looked at each other and I could see we were all frightened. Someone said that on this day's selection we were all going to be taken. Nobody was to remain from our barracks. It created such a panic that everyone started to run and hide.

I ran into a storage room that was full of bundles of clothing waiting to be deloused. I squeezed myself between some of the bundles, and two or three other girls tried to squeeze themselves next to me. Wherever one person ran others would follow. Like frightened children we would run and try to hide. I grabbed some dirty clothes that were nearby. I saw that the clothes were full of lice, but I was so frightened of the selection that I covered myself with the clothes anyway.

One girl ran and hid in the chimney. Two other girls tried to get in behind her and pushed her up the chimney. The Germans chased after all of us and dragged us out of our hiding places. When the three girls were pulled out of the chimney they were as black as chimney sweeps. The Germans laughed as hard as they could after looking at those three girls.

The Lagerfearer then came in and shouted at us and said, "What is going on here? Aren't you healthy enough to work?"

Then we saw there was going to be a selection after all. We started to calm down. We saw that there was still a chance to live. A fifty percent chance to live was better than none. We lined up for the selection.

At that time a lot of us had lice. The Germans were beginning to delouse us, and our barracks. At that selection we looked like we had leprosy.

The rumor about all of us going to the gas chamber started because of the lice infestation. To combat the infestation the Germans took a whole barracks of women and sent them to the gas chamber without a selection. They deloused that group's barracks. Then they deloused the women from the next barracks. Those women were moved into the deloused barracks and their old barracks were then deloused. This went on throughout the camp. My group was two barracks away from the group that went to the gas chamber.

This was in the winter at the end of 1943. At that selection the Lagerfearer stood there, with a few other Germans, watching the selection. As I passed the doctor I saw him mention to Eticha to record my number.

During a selection a lot of girls would try to get past the doctor as fast as they could. Sometimes the whole row of us would get out of order when someone tried to run past the doctor. Just as Etichka started to write down my number the girl behind me started to run past me. The doctor, seeing her start to run, grabbed her and pushed her back into line. During the commotion I looked at Etichka, and she motioned, with her head for me to quickly leave. She was also a Jewish child and would look for opportunities to help us. I stepped around the doctor as he was pushing the other girl and left the room. Eticha did not write down my number.

There were selections often in Auschwitz. Sometimes we would know about them the day before. If in the evening we heard that the next day there was going to be a selection many of us cried all night.

One night before a selection I dreamed of my grandparents. In the dream they started naming relatives of mine that I had never met, but knew by name. My Grandfather said to me in my dream, "Don't be afraid because your whole family is praying for you. You'll pass the selection."

And it happened that way. The next day's selection I did pass. After that the same dream came to me before another selection. I did not fear that selection because of the dream.

In Auschwitz I would often dream about my home. It's interesting that in that hell many of my dreams were quite pleasant. I would tell everyone that I lived for those dreams. The time I was awake was the real nightmare.

There was an open field between the fence and our barracks. Sometimes the Germans left groups of people there, who just got off a transport, over night. One night I heard that the people in the field were from the Lodz ghetto. This was at the end of the summer in 1944. The Lodz ghetto was being emptied then. I crawled out of my barracks and crawled over to the group. I had to crawl so as not to be seen by the guard. I moved among them asking if anyone was from Boleslawiec. One lady answered that she was from a town nearby and had family in Boleslawiec. I knew her family well. Their name was Kasril.

She said she was cold. So I crawled back to my barracks and brought her a blanket. She must have been very tired from the transport so we did not talk. There was nothing to tell them because they all knew about Auschwitz by this time. I returned to my barracks, and by the morning the lady and the rest of the people in the field were gone.

Another time, around September 1944, I heard about another group that had arrived from the Lodz ghetto. I heard it was a group of women and that they were at the Sauna. I went over and walked around the edge of the area making sure no Germans saw me. I called to a group of women standing outside the door to the Sauna asking if anyone was from

Wielun or Boleslawiec. A girl, wrapped in a blanket, called out that she was. She turned out to be my cousin Jizka Krzepizka. With her was her younger sister Yenta. They had been sent to work, as seamstresses, in the Lodz ghetto during the last round up of Jews from our hometown.

We were only able to talk for a minute or two. They had to go into the Sauna, and I had to hurry away. Jizka and Yenta did not remain in Auschwitz, but were sent on to Stuttgart where they worked until the liberation.

So much happened in Auschwitz. I remember a mother and daughter who lived together in the same barracks. They were from Lodz. When they came to take the mother away, when she did not pass a selection, her daughter grabbed on to her and would not let go. I saw them pulled apart by the soldiers who came for the mother. As the mother was led away the daughter had to be held down. They called each other's name over and over. All of us who watched couldn't help but cry.

Another woman was there in our barracks with her two daughters. They all worked together on the 103rd Kommaddo. Once we were working in the gravel quarry, called the kise gruben. I was digging out the small stones, and the woman and her two daughters were carrying what we called a tragga. It was like a wheel barrel without the wheels. Instead it had 4 handles and was carried by 4 people between the quarry and where the road was being built. When it was full of stones it was very heavy.

Returning from delivering a load of stones the woman and her daughters stopped by me and set their tragga down for me to fill it. While it was being filled they had a chance to rest. As I was filling it one of the daughters asked if I would trade places with her mother. Digging the stones was easier work then carrying the loaded tragga. I looked at the woman. She reminded me of my mother. I could not refuse.

Another time a group of us was working in the quarry. This was before I found the money in the skirt. A German in a barracks next to the quarry was watching us. He called over a few of his friends. As they watched he threw a tomato into our group. We all jumped at the tomato at once and crushed it. No one got any of it, but the Germans had a good laugh. It was a comedy to them.

Before I found the money I was always hungry. Once I hid outside a barracks the Germans lived in. I waited for them to throw out their garbage which they did every day after supper. After they threw it out, I picked through it and found cabbage leaves and some potato peels. I ate anything that looked like it could be eaten. A lot of us would do this every day. There was a lot of hunger there.

Once I was standing outside of our barracks with a woman named Frana. She lived in the same section of the barracks as I did. I never did know her last name. Most of us did not know each other's last names. I do remember that she was from Lodz. We knew that she had not passed the last selection. She knew that in the morning they would come for her. I asked her if there was anything that she wanted. She said, "Mala, if you have some extra food I would like to have it. I would like to not feel hungry when they come for me in the morning."

I had some bread and some margarine. I gave it to her, and she ate it. Eating calmed her down, and in the morning she went without a fuss.

I remember the time I was late getting to the Appel. During the Appel everyone in the camp was suppose to line up in front of their barracks. This was on a Sunday. Many

Sundays were called Arbeitssonntags, which meant working Sundays. We worked on those days till 1 P.M., and then we had a roll call. Each barracks would line up and be counted. All our numbers would be checked against a list. The whole camp stayed on the Appel until all the barracks were counted.

After work on that day I went to the Rewier to trade among the sick. I was living in Lager B, and the Rewier was in Lager A. Only a fence and a gate separated the two camps. I had forgotten that there was to be an Appel that day.

While I was in the Rewier I stopped to talk to some of the girls who were sick there. As I was sitting there talking to someone, a nurse walked in and saw me. At the top of her voice she said to me, "You are here? You Shumstick, They've been searching for you for over two hours."

We were often called Shumsticks by the more privileged of the inmates. In German it meant a small item with only sentimental value. Sometimes they called us musselmen, which was worse. Musselman meant you were so thin that you were only good for the gas chamber.

During the roll call of my barracks I was found missing. For over two hours all the girls of Lager B were kept standing on the Appel as the Blockalteste went looking for me. When I heard this from the nurse, I grabbed my things and ran out of the Rewier.

The distance between the Rewier in Lager A and my barracks in Lager B was a 10-minute walk. I ran through the gate separating the two lagers. Everyone lined up on the Appel watched me as I ran over. I had to run past a group of SS. As I approached, an SS woman, named Drexler, stepped in front of me and hit me in the face. She hit me so hard that I was knocked to the ground. On my hands and knees I tried to get around her, but she grabbed hold of me and continued to beat me. She was hitting me with all her strength. After a few seconds I got out of her grasp and ran as fast as I could over to my group.

When I got to my group, my Blockalteste, Etta started hitting me. After Etta hit me a few times Etichka said to her, "Let her go already. See how she looks. Her whole head and face are bleeding. Leave her alone."

Etta let me go and I ran into my row so they could finish the Appel. As soon as it was over I ran into my barracks. I ran into the corner of the barracks. I was too afraid to move and didn't even go out to eat. I stayed there, in the corner, for the rest of the day. By the morning I felt that everything had calmed down, and I went back to work with everyone else.

10
AUSCHWITZ, AT THE END

By the summer of 1944 the Germans started evacuating Auschwitz. Every day they would empty more and more of Birkenau. Every day I could see transports full of people and things leaving the camp.

Everyone talked about the Russian front. Every day there were reports on its movements through Poland. People were already talking about a liberation. We knew that the war was going badly for the Germans, but nobody knew for sure what was happening. Everything was just rumors. One day we would hear one story, and the next we would hear just the opposite.

By the end of the summer we heard that the crematoriums were being dismantled. There were five crematoriums, and the Germans dismantled four of them. It was also announced that there would be no more selections. The one remaining crematorium was to be used for those who died of natural causes.

To us the news of no more selections was like hearing that the Messiah had come. We walked around kissing each other and wishing Mazel Tov to every one we saw. What we were really congratulating each other on was surviving.

At the end of the summer 1944 our kommando, the 103rd, was dismantled. All the buildings that we built in Birkenau were by then destroyed by Allied bombardments. The only work for us was to clear away the rubble. There was a rumor that the members of our kommando were going to be evacuated to Germany by truck. I was afraid to go. Some said that the trucks use in the evacuations were the kind of trucks used to kill people before the gas chambers were built. The people who were loaded into the trucks were gassed with the engine exhaust as the truck moved. But I was wrong. The people who left the camp at this time did go to other camps in Germany.

After the war my sister, Fay, told me about the time she found out that I was in Auschwitz. Fay was in a labor camp in Germany called Langinbello. She worked there as a seamstress. There she met a woman who thought Fay was me. The woman was evacuated from Auschwitz at the time I was afraid to go. She ended up in the work camp with my sister. She came over to my sister and started talking to her as if she was talking to me. When we were children, people were always confusing my sister Fay and me. That was when Fay knew I was alive and in Auschwitz.

I had a friend in camp named Lutka Moskowitz. She was from Dabrowa, near Sosnowiec. Today she lives in Israel. She also worked in the 103rd Kommando, and was one of the nine other girls that stood with me in a row on the Appel. We helped each other with our tradings. Sometimes I would arrange a trade for her, and sometimes she would arrange one for me. We would arrange to pick things up for each other. We helped each other when we could. She also kept an assistant to help her just like Rose Etta helped me.

Lutka also feared the evacuation of our kommando. We talked about what we should do to make sure that we stayed in Auschwitz. We decided to try and bribe the Arbeitsensatz. The Arbeitsensatz was a German who assigned the women in the camp to the different jobs. We were going to bribe her to get a job that was indoors. At that time only the Ausser Kommandos were being evacuated.

We learned that she was a drinker. We got a couple of things of value together and traded them on the kommando for a bottle of whiskey. I carried it back into the camp under my jacket.

At first we were afraid to go to her directly so we went to a Jewish assistant of hers. We told the assistant that we wanted to see the Arbeitsensatz and showed her the bottle of whiskey. We told her we wanted to trade the whiskey for jobs in the Blue Affect. We had a friend who worked there, and we knew that we could find things there to trade. The assistant picked up the bottle of whiskey, gave it a shake, and handed it back to me. She said that the Arbeitsensatz demanded very clean whiskey, and ours wasn't clean enough for her. She sent us away saying she couldn't help us.

This was a great blow to us. We had traded all our valuables for that bottle. Just getting that bottle of whiskey proved to be very difficult. Getting another one that was cleaner we knew would be impossible.

I was heartbroken, but Lutka decided not to give up. She said that we should take a chance and go directly to the Arbeitsensatz. She figured that if she was a drinker she would take the whiskey anyway. So that's what we did.

The Arbeitsensatz's name was Katka. She was a German political prisoner. We went to the barracks where her office was. When we got there the Blockalteste of that barracks asked us what we wanted. We told her we wanted to see Katka, and that we had something for her. She had us wait outside and went in to see if Katka would see us. A minute later she returned and let us in.

We came in to Katka's office and walked up to her desk. I said to her, "Gutten tag," and pulled out the bottle of whiskey.

I placed it on her desk. First she looked at the bottle and then at us. She said, "What do you want my children?"

By the sound of her voice I knew we had her.

I told her that we had been working in the Ausser Kommando already for over 15 months. We felt that it was time we were allowed to work under a roof. She asked, "Where do you want to go?"

"Kommando 105, the Blue Affect."

"Good, more workers are needed for the 105th Kommando."

Since they were liquidating the camp there was more to do at the Blue Affect. She said she was going to assign ten more women to the Blue Affect. We asked her not to assign anyone yet. We would give her a list of the numbers of 8 friends of ours to assign with us to Kommando 105.

She said, "Fine, give me the list in the morning as you leave the camp for work."

Every morning she stood at the gate to the camp counting the workers as they left. The workers marched five to a row. She was handed a list of ten numbers every second row. She told me to make sure that our ten numbers were on one list and that I should hand it to her.

The next morning we did as she told us. That evening Lutka and I went to see her. She said that she was able to only assign 8 women to the 105th Kommando, and she had removed our 2 numbers from the list. We started crying and asked her why she had removed our numbers. She looked at us and said, "Which two other numbers should I remove from the list?"

Lutka and I looked at each other. We didn't want to remove anybody else's number because we were sure it meant their death if we did.

We continued to beg her to restore our two numbers and try to get us into Kommando 105. We promised her that the girls would get together and pay her whatever she wanted. She said that she would see what she could do.

Over the next few days the ten of us brought her whatever we could. We brought her fruit and jewelry, everything we could get our hands on. A week later all ten of us were assigned to the Blue Affect.

The Blue Affect was in the city of Auschwitz, not in the camp. Every member of this kommando had to wear a blue kerchief on their heads at all times. This was where the clothes that were taken away from the people who were killed in the gas chamber were sorted. There were piles and piles of clothing taken from the millions of people who came to Auschwitz.

The Blue Affect was in a building called the Leather Factory. It was a two story high building. Our kommando worked on the second floor. Downstairs was a laundry for the SS. There were a number of other factory buildings around it.

First, all the victim's items and clothes were sent to a kommando called the Canada. It was called the Canada because, like the real Canada, it was a land of plenty. The longest surviving inmates in Auschwitz worked there. It was the best place in the camp. It took a lot of bribery and good connections to get a job there. Then the clothing was brought to the Blue Affect. Our job was to separate the different kinds of items. Coats to coats, socks to socks, like that. Then we further separated them according to the material they were made of. Last we would wrap the piles of clothing and pack them for shipment.

As we sorted the items we would check for hidden things. Since I found the money in the skirt I carefully felt every piece of clothing I touched. Once I found a gold ring with two small diamonds in it, in a sock. I still have that ring. The most useful item I took from the Blue Affect was a pair of shoes. They didn't fit perfectly, but at least I again had a pair of real shoes. Another thing I remember keeping was a small prayer book that I was able to hide in my pocket.

The head of our kommando was called the Shef, which meant master or boss. He was a man who drank a lot. He wore a green SS uniform, and when he was drunk he was a terror. And he was drunk quite often. At times he would stagger among us drunk and would start beating one of us for no reason at all.

Sometimes for fun he would sit himself on a pile of clothing. He would make us line up and march past him as he hit us. Once he took a liking to one of the girls. He walked up to her, and in front of all of us, grabbed her. As he tried to kiss her he put his hand up her dress. She struggled with him until he became angry. He then started beating her. He beat her for so long that when he stopped she was almost dead.

At the end of the day's work he would tell us to get ready to leave. He would go outside as we put on our coats. We would stand around and wait for him to call us outside. Outside we would line up, be counted, and marched back to our camp.

Once, while we were waiting for him to call us, I sat down next to one of the tables. I leaned my head against the wall and fell asleep. While I was asleep he called us outside. Everyone went out without me. After counting the other women he came back looking for me.

I woke up hearing him come screaming into the room. He came over to me and started kicking me. I got up and ran out of the building with him running and cursing behind me. The other girls were lined up outside. I ran in and lined up among the other girls. By the time he came out of the building I was already standing in one of the rows. He didn't know where to find me. I'm sure he was drunk, and we all probably looked alike to him. He looked around for a minute. Once he even stared straight at me. After awhile he gave up and let us go back to our camp.

I only worked in the 105th Kommando for a short while. After a few weeks the Blue Affect was also liquidated. The pace of the evacuation was speeding up. Most of our kommando, with a thousand other women, was taken into the main section of Auschwitz and put into a compound. I got separated from Sala and Rose Etta. They were part of a group that was sent to another camp.

Our new compound was a group of brick buildings. One of the buildings was called Block 1. Block 1 was where the Germans performed experiments on prisoners. We had heard about Block 1 before. A lot of women that came to Berkinau were first in Block 1. In the toilets, where 20 or 30 of us could go into at the same time, the women from Block 1 would show us their scars. The women were mostly young Greek Jews, girls really, 16 to 17 years old. I remember them having large dark eyes. They were very beautiful. The scars they showed us were large cuts across their stomachs. The experiments left them sterile.

Block 1 also housed the camp's women's band. I was only there once. It was during Christmas at the end of 1944. The band put on a play and a concert for the SS. They allowed any of the women in the camp to come. The play was in German, and the SS seemed to enjoy it very much.

The group of women I was with was assigned to Blocks 2, 3, 4 and 5. This was in the last few months of 1944. I was assigned to a kommando called the Davu. The Davu's job was to rebuild some of the buildings and roads around the camp. The men worked as carpenters on the buildings. I was in a group of about 30 women working on repairing the roads. It wasn't a large kommando.

The work of repairing the roads involved setting new stones and clearing away the old ones. After a few days of working there, the German overseer came and watched us work. I had done this kind of work in Birkenau and knew how the stones needed to be set. I knew that the points of the stones were to be set on top. That smaller stones were to go between the larger ones, and then the cement was to go over the smaller stones. Building roads was some of the work we did on the 103rd Kommando.

After watching me work for a while the Shef, who was the German head of our kommando asked me, "How do you know how to do this work so well?"

I told him of my work in the 103rd Kommando. He told me to stop working and to teach the other women how to do it. I was to be the Anviser, which meant trainer.

After a few days of teaching the other girls how to lay the stones, I was made the Vorarbeiter of our group. After that the Shef was hardly there. After he got us started in the morning, he would go away and return only once in awhile. When he left we would set someone up to watch for his return. We took it slowly until we heard the signal that he was coming. When we saw him coming we would signal by shouting, "Six." Then we would make ourselves look very busy. He always returned around lunchtime. I always made a big fuss about how hard my girls were working and tried to get extra soup for them and an extra sausage. Most of the time we would get it.

After the war, in Germany, I met a woman named Edga Hecht. Once we were talking about where we had been during the war. We learned that we were both in Auschwitz at the same time. Before Auschwitz she was in a camp called Plachofka, near Krakow. She mentioned about working in Auschwitz on the Davu. When I heard her say the Davu I said, "You worked in the Davu? I also worked there."

This was two years after the war and we looked quite different than we had looked in Auschwitz.

Edga asked, "What work did you do there?"

I said, "Don't you recognize me? I'm Mala. I was your Vorarbeiter."

We were so thrilled to find each other. She took me around to all the other people she knew, telling them the stories about us looking out for the Overseer and the extra rations of soup. We became very close friends and are friends to this day. She led me down the aisle and under the Chuppa at my wedding in Wiesbaden in 1947.

One day on the Davu, a friend of Alter's, from home, came to see me. His name was Mosha Lefkowitz. Today Mosha lives in Israel. He brought me some sausage. After that, every week or so, he would sent a package of food with a friend who worked near our section.

One morning, after working on the Davu for about 6 weeks, our barracks was inspected by a SS woman. Our barracks was a new one with two floors. The top floor was for sleeping, and on the bottom were long tables for eating. It had been recently constructed and was used as a showpiece for the Red Cross. So the SS frequently inspected it.

The SS woman stopped at my bed and inspected the sheet. She turned to me and said that she liked the way I made my bed. She appointed me a Sthoubova, a section leader. She told me that I was not to go to work any more but to remain in the barracks. My job was to clean and straighten up when the other girls left for work in the morning. The girls made their own beds, but I was to straighten them out and fix the corners after they left.

My work also included going to the kitchen and bringing the food to our barracks, giving out the food when the girls returned from work, and returning the pots to the kitchen after they had eaten. My job was a privileged position since it was winter and the work, except for getting the food, was all indoors.

It was at this time, while I was a Sthoubova, that the girls from the Union were hanged. I had to witness the morning hanging since I didn't leave the camp for work and the evening one since my barracks was lined up to see it.

In October 1944, a short while after I was transferred to the main camp at Auschwitz, the uprising in Birkenau happened. The men who worked around the gas chambers and the crematoriums were called the Sonderkommandos. Every few months the Germans would send the Sonderkommandos into the gas chamber and replace them with new men.

The Sonderkommandos had gotten a cache of weapons. When the Germans tried to send them into the gas chambers they rose up against the Germans. They killed a few Germans, blew up one of the crematoriums, and tore down part of the fence around the camp. Some of the girls in Birkenau escaped through the hole in the fence.

But the uprising didn't last long. Soon the Germans put it down and caught the escapees. After torturing the

Sonderkommandos, the Germans learned that they had gotten the weapons from some of the girls who worked in the Union.

The Union was the ammunitions factory in Auschwitz. Over 2000 men and women from the camp worked there in two shifts, one by day and the other by night. Some of the workers smuggled out explosives for the men in the Sonderkommando.

The Germans took all of the women who worked in the Union into the Sauna. There were over a thousand of them. Among them was a girl from my town named Hinga. She was one of the 30 girls who were taken at the same time as my sisters. Hinga and Rose Etta were the only survivors of those 30 girls.

The Germans threatened to send all the women from the Union to the gas chamber if the guilty ones didn't come forward. They were questioned and beaten till the Germans found the four girls who were involved in smuggling the explosives.

After the uprising was suppressed the Germans made us line up on the square. We were surrounded by a couple of hundred Germans. They had their guns aimed at us in case we should start an uprising too. The Germans made a speech. I don't remember what they said. All I remember was looking at those two girls. We had to watch as they were hung.

At night the other two girls were hung for the day workers to watch. We heard that six men were also hung in front of the men's camp. That was the end of the uprising in Auschwitz.

When I hear people say that the Jews went to their deaths like sheep I get very upset. I saw many acts of courage and defiance by Jews against the Germans, but they always ended in death. Everybody did what they could to rescue themselves.

At the beginning we never imagined the horror of our situation. By the time we did the Jews weren't organized to do anything against the Germans. Before the Germans killed, they lied. As the Germans were sending the people to their deaths they were telling them that they were going to be resettled. As the Germans were about to gas the people they would tell them they were just going to have a shower. People didn't want to believe that they were about to die so they believed the lies.

And who did the Germans march to their deaths? The old, the children, the sick, and ones who lost the will to live because of what the Germans did to them. The young and the strong rose up against the Germans when they could. But the Germans were a mighty nation with an army that almost conquered the world. What were we Jews? Without a country, without weapons, and without anyone to defend us. The Germans murdered and killed and nobody came to our aid. It was a big miracle that any of us remained alive at all.

Around this time I had a visit from a man from my hometown. His name was Baruch Traugutt. In 1941, while I was still at home, the Germans arrested him for selling coal on the black market. His boss at the time was a German named Weis. Weis' family lived in our town. His parents owned the local water mill. Weis was only allowed to sell the coal to people with ration cards, and only a certain amount. But he did a big business on the black market. Weis was the one the Germans caught, but he put all the blame on Baruch, his worker. As a German he was given very favorable treatment, so they punished his worker instead of him.

At home we all thought the Germans had killed Baruch. Even his parents thought so. They were never able to get any information about him from the Germans. It turned out that he was sent to Auschwitz as a criminal. He wore a green triangle on his jacket. The Jews wore a yellow one. As a criminal inmate he received better treatment than the Jewish ones.

He had heard that some of the women sent from Birkenau to the Auschwitz main camp were from his hometown. He bribed a Kapo to be included in a work detail that came into the women's section. The work detail came regularly into our section to clean out the sewers.

He came into our barracks and saw me. He called my name. I looked at him for a minute not knowing who he was. Then I recognized him. I called his name and ran up to him. We hugged. I told him how I thought he was dead, that everyone thought so. I was so happy to see him. He had brought me a small cake. He gave it to me and said, "I have some news that will make you even happier."

The news he brought me was about my husband Alter. Around the time I came to Birkenau from Majdanek, Alter also came to Auschwitz. Baruch had seen him and talked to him. Alter was now working in a coalmine not far from Auschwitz. Baruch said he would try to get word to him about me. Later he would try to smuggle a letter for me.

Baruch also saw a number of other people from our town. He told me what he knew about some of my cousins that were also in Auschwitz. I asked him if he knew anything about my younger brother Wolf. I had heard nothing about him since his escape from the camp in Posnan. Alter was with him in that camp. I asked him if Alter had said anything about my brother. He said he had heard nothing about Wolf. But I felt he wasn't telling me the truth. After the war I found out that he did indeed know but chose not to tell me.

We were only able to talk for a short while, 15 or 20 minutes. He had to get back to the work detail. He said he would be back as soon as he could, but I never saw Baruch again in Auschwitz. I did see him after the war in America. He did not go back to our hometown after he was liberated. Today he lives in Miami.

The evacuation took place soon after his visit.

My work as a Sthoubova lasted about 7 weeks until January 18, 1945. On the evening of the 17th we were each given a whole loaf of bread and a blanket and told that in the morning we were going to be evacuated from Auschwitz. Nobody would tell us where we were going only that we were leaving. There were all kinds of rumors, and we were all very afraid. It was cold and there was deep snow outside. We had seen other columns of people march off into the snow and were never heard from again.

Everybody collected rags and wrapped up their feet for the walk through the snow. I also had a pair of socks that I took from the Blue Affect. I collected some of my things. We were each given a loaf of bread and a wool blanket. All the rest of the things I had fit in my pockets.

It was hard to sleep that night as we waited for the morning.

11
DEATH MARCH AND THE LAST CAMPS

In the morning, January 18, 1945, we were awakened and rushed out of our barracks. From all around us I could see people coming out and lining up in front of their barracks. We all looked the same with rags around our feet and blankets over our heads. Then barrack-by-barrack we were marched out of the camp. Thousands of people formed a long column. Every few feet on both sides of the column walked a German soldier with a gun.

It was a cold January day. We couldn't walk very fast. Many of us were weak, but nobody wanted to go to the Rewier. We were sure that the sick in the Rewier would be killed. We were sure that the Germans would not leave them to be found by the Russians. But they weren't killed. They were the first of the inmates of Auschwitz to be liberated. Nine days after we left, the Russians arrived.

The snow outside the camp was very deep. When I stepped out of where the column was walking the snow was up to my knees. The Germans ordered us always to go faster. Within a day or two, those that weren't going fast enough or had stopped altogether were shot. The people near the ones that had been shot were ordered to pull the body to the side of the road so it would not be in the way of the rest of the column.

Hundreds were killed. I could hear shooting going on constantly up and down the column. We walked between rows of dead on both sides of us. As the march dragged on the rows of dead seemed endless.

In the distance we could hear the dull thuds of the bombardments on the front and see the flashes on the horizon. The explosions and the flashes never stopped. I could feel them getting nearer. That sound of the Russian guns drove the Germans just as the sound of their shooting drove us.

The days were very cold and each day it seemed to get colder. The Germans also suffered from the cold and the walking. They took their suffering out on us. Some drank a lot to fight the cold. I saw many of them drunk and watched some just shoot into the column at random. They would curse us as if it was our doing that they were out in the cold.

We walked for days, and sometimes the nights too. I lost track of time. A couple of times during each day the column would stop. Not for us to rest but because of something that was happening in front of us. Sometimes we would be allowed to sit and sometimes not. I remember the Germans seeming very nervous during these stops. After awhile we would be ordered to move again. There were those who could not move. The Germans just shot them where they lay.

Most of the nights we were allowed to rest, but always in the open. We would sit in the snow and lean against each other and try to sleep. At night the Germans were afraid we would escape so we were put in groups and watched from all sides.

We walked through woods and on small country roads. We always walked around towns, never through them, even if it meant a longer walk. It seemed like the Germans were hiding us from the people along the way. In the woods we did walk past some houses. Sometimes people would come out to see us. Our guards discouraged their curiosity and would not let them talk to us or us to them.

We must have been a sight to the people who saw us. I saw some stare at us out of curiosity and some look at us with pity. And some I saw close their curtains as we passed. I was told by some of the other marchers that some people who lived along the way did throw food and give out some blankets to the marchers.

At the start of the march I walked with Lutka, Reginka and Shindala. I saw my Greek friend Stella. We walked together for a while and then I lost her. I never saw her again.

A few days into the march we lost Lutka. She was able to hide in the attic of a barn. She was able to stay there until the Russians came a few days later. I didn't know what happened to her until I got home to Boleslawiec. There in the city hall I found a letter from her looking for information about me.

During the rest stops we were able to walk up and down the column. I walked around looking for Alter and my brother Wolf, or anyone who knew anything about them. I though Wolf was still alive then and had come to Auschwitz with Alter.

After about 10 to 12 days, I don't remember exactly how many, of what seemed like aimlessly wandering around, we came to the labor camp at Gross Rosen. Gross Rosen was about 200 miles from Auschwitz. There the Germans were suppose to leave us but found that labor camp also in the process of evacuating. When we came into the camp I thought at last we'd be able to go indoors and maybe get some food. But soon after we got there we were ordered to leave again. There didn't seem any place for us but the snow.

That day I remember a terrible frost setting in. After we left Gross Rosen I felt like giving up. The thought of walking again through the woods in that cold and snow was too much for me. I was ready to lie down and accept my fate. That's when Shindala and Raginka saved my life as I already told.

We walked for the rest of the day. In the evening we were allowed to rest in a barn. The barn was very big, and hundreds of us rested there. Lying on the straw I regained my strength and my will to live.

The next morning we were ordered out of the barn. We marched a short distance to where a train was waiting for us. We were loaded onto open rail wagons for the rest of our journey.

The train traveled very slowly. It stopped and started many times. The trip lasted a few days. I can't recall exactly how many because time wasn't our main concern. Food was. Time was figured from when we last ate. Hunger and cold were our only thoughts. Traveling in open wagons in winter all we did was huddle against the wind and cold.

When the train did stop we were allowed to get out of the wagons and relieve ourselves at the side of the tracks. Once when I was relieving myself at the side of the wagon the train started moving without warning. The Germans were shooting anyone who did not get back on the train. With my pants hardly pulled up I started running and tried to grab onto the ladder of the wagon. One of the girls in the wagon reached out and grabbed my arm. Then a few more hands grabbed mine and pulled me off my feet. As the train moved faster and faster my body dangled on the side of the wagon. Everybody in the wagon seemed to grab hold of me, and together they pulled me in. Without their help I never would have made it into the wagon.

After the war when I was living in Brooklyn, I was visiting a neighbor. The neighbor had a friend of hers visiting at the same time. The neighbor and her friend were also survivors. So we sat around and told stories of the war. I told them the story of being pulled into the train. The neighbor's friend, her name was Ava Munlach, clapped her hands and gave out a loud laugh. She said, "Oh, it was you. I'm the one who first grabbed your hand as you ran for the train. For years I thought about that and wondered what happened to you."

So 8 years after it happened I got the chance to thank my rescuer.

During the trip we pulled into a train station. The train stopped there for the longest time. All around us were piles of rubble. There was hardly a building intact. Some people walked by, and we begged them for food. We hadn't eaten for days and that was all we thought about. The guards would threaten us to get us to stop pleading and would tell the onlookers to move. The people passing by would look at us in amazement. Some would cross themselves. Someone in the wagon shouted to a passerby, "Where are we?"

The reply was, "Berlin."

We all fell silent as we looked around. It hardly looked like a city at all, let alone the capital of the Reich. There were mounds of rubble and just the skeletons of buildings as far as the eye could see.

Over the station's loudspeaker a man's voice kept saying over and over again, "Apfahren mit dem sou laden. Apfahren mit dem sou laden."

After awhile I realized he meant our train. What he kept saying was, "Away with the pig train."

The train finally came to its destination, the women's labor camp at Ravensbruck. The camp was very big and in great turmoil. An endless stream of trucks and people, moving in and out of the camp. Transports were arriving from all over with inmates from camps in Poland. We were more crowded there than we were in Auschwitz,

The camp leaders at Ravensbruck (they were also inmates) were Christians from Czechoslovakia. The Germans there behaved better since the war seemed lost. Suddenly they weren't so bad to the Jews. Some would even tell us how good they had been. I was not used to this kind of behavior from the Germans.

We stayed in Ravensbruck for about 2 weeks. From there the people were dispatched to other labor camps in Germany. Most of the time we were left alone because there was nothing for us to do. But those that didn't have work also got very little food. One morning Shindala came into our barracks dragging a whole kettle of soup. We didn't ask how she got it. We all gathered around and shared that pot of soup. It was the first warm food we had since leaving Auschwitz.

I ran into a girl named Hadasa. Even though she was Jewish she had had a privileged position in Auschwitz. She was an assistant to a Kapo from the 103rd Kommando. But here in Ravensbruck she was in the same position as the rest of us.

In Auschwitz I had received many beatings from Hadasa. Not just me but all of us in the kommando. Once she caught me in the toilet. She beat me until I was black and blue. It was because she had seen me switch groups during work so I could do some trading.

I warned her that if she were around when we were set free we'd pay her back for all those beatings. She made sure she wasn't sent to the same camp as we were.

Years later in New York, Sala told me she had seen Hadasa. Sala was traveling on a bus and saw Hadasa walking on the street. Sala started yelling and banging on the window. She got off at the next stop and ran back to where she had seen her. But she was gone and Sala couldn't find her.

One morning I was included in a group of about 4000 women that were taken to the train. We had all come from Auschwitz together. We were put into closed wagons, 45 women to a wagon. When they loaded us there was no bullying or hitting, and we weren't crammed into the wagons. The treatment was almost gentle. There was a rumor that we were being sent to Sweden as part of a prisoner exchange.

Sweden was not our destination. Instead we were brought to a labor camp called Neustadt Glewe. It was on the river Elbe. The camp was in the woods, almost half way between Berlin and Hamburg. The workers in the camp worked in a nearby airplane factory that was hidden in the woods. It was a small camp, only about 4000 inmates were housed there.

When we first arrived, there were no barracks for us to stay in. We were put in a large empty building with straw spread out on the floor. We were to replace the 4000 women who were then working there. Those 4000 women were prisoners from the Polish uprising in Warsaw. We had to wait till they were removed. We were given our food ration for the day. Those not assigned to a work detail were given one slice of bread and a half a glass of soup. That's what we were supposed to live on.

The first evening in Neustadt, as I lay on the straw, someone reminded me that it was Friday and that the Sabbath was about to begin. I had never lost my faith in God. I still had in my pocket a small prayer book that I had found in Auschwitz. I took it out and started reciting the Friday evening prayer. Sitting next to me was a woman. I can't remember her name, but I remember she was from Sosnowiec. She started laughing at me. She said to the others, "Look, she still believes in prayer."

Then she started making fun of me. As soon as I was finished praying I got up and left the building. I did not want to listen to her anymore.

Shindala walked out of the building with me. She suggested we check out the camp. Since they were going to organize us into work details, Shindala suggested we find out about the kitchens and the laundry. We knew from experience that they were the best places to work. Shindala had a small gold ring on her. She was going to use it to get a job in one of those places.

As long as we stayed in the camp we were allowed to wander around. I saw a commotion in front of one of the barracks nearby so I wandered over to it. In front of the barracks I found one of the Lagerelteste selecting women for work details.

I heard her select some of the women for work in the laundry. I walked up to her and stood in front of her. She looked at me and asked me what I wanted. I told her I wanted to work in the laundry. She said, "I have enough. I don't need anymore."

She lined up the women she had selected and marched them to the other side of the camp. The barracks on that side of the camp were for the SS. One of the buildings housed the SS kitchen and their laundry.

I followed them across the camp. When they got to the other side, they were divided up into groups for the different jobs, and shown to Drexler. Drexler was now one of the SS camp leaders. She was one of the worst Lagerfearers in Auschwitz. She was the one that beat me when I was late for an Appel.

Some of the girls were assigned to the kitchens, some to the laundry, and some to cleaning the toilets. I walk up to

Drexler and stood next to her. She looked at me and asked, "What do you want?"

I told her that I had worked in Auschwitz in the laundry and that the SS women there were very happy with my work. I told her that I wished to work in the laundry.

I knew that in the laundry I would have it the best. It would be warm in there, and the work wouldn't be that hard. And since it was in the same building as the kitchen I would be able to get some extra food.

Standing next to Drexler was my old Blockelteste from Auschwitz, Etta Locks. Etta was one of the women picked by the Lagerfearer for one of her details. She turned to the Lagerfearer and told her that it was true that my work in the laundry in Auschwitz was very good. Why she lied to help me I don't know, but the Lagerfearer relented and told me to join the group assigned to the laundry.

I don't know what happened to Etta Locks at the end of the war. When the Russians came into the camp some of the Russian inmates pointed out the collaborators among the other inmates. Because of her work as a Blockalteste in Auschwitz she was pointed out and taken into custody.

From a distance Shindala watched all of this. As I went to stand with the other women from the laundry I saw Shindala gesture to me as if saying what should she do. I motioned to her to do as I did. The Lagerfearer wasn't hitting anyone, so she should try. Shindala came over and asked to also be assigned to the laundry. The Lagerfearer just nodded okay, and told her to stand with me.

Drexler's behavior in this camp was a lot different than it was in Auschwitz. Since she knew that the end was near I think she thought about how she would be treated by the victors.

Our group and the other women who were assigned work in the kitchens and the toilets were housed together in one barracks. Our rations were now 2 quarts of soup and 2 pieces of bread a day. A few days later the other women, who came with me from Ravensburck, were assigned work in the airplane factory. They were all housed together in a group of barracks at the other end of the camp.

Some of the other girls in the laundry with me were Shindala, Chesha Koplowitz and Sonia. Chesha was from Lodz. Sonia shared a bunk with me in Neustadt. Today Sonia lives in Arizona.

Our work in the laundry gave us access to extra food and the only hot water in the camp. The laundry and the kitchen were in the same building. The girls who worked in the kitchen were searched after work so they could not smuggle out any food. The girls from the laundry had to go to get wood to heat the large pots of water that we did our cleaning in. The woodpile was near the entrance to the kitchen. We arranged with the kitchen staff that when we went for wood they would slip us some food. We were not searched when we left work so we were able to bring the food back to our barracks. Then it was shared between the two groups.

Since it was still winter, only by coming to the laundry were the girls able to get some warm water. This way they were at least able to wash themselves, even if it was just their hands and faces and maybe their heads. All day in small groups the girls sneaked over to the laundry. They would come to the window and call for some water. We would make sure nobody was looking and hand them a pot of hot water and a little bit of soap.

Not far from our camp was a men's camp called Neuengamme. The other women would meet some of the men from that camp while they worked in the airplane factory. Every time inmates from the two camps met they would list the names of the other people in their camps. That was how I found out that a cousin and an in-law of mine were in Neuengamme. The Germans killed them before they were liberated. They were among the inmates that the Germans put on a ship and sunk in the river Elbe right before Neuengamme was liberated.

One day there was a rumor that our camp was going to be evacuated. After our last experience it caused a great deal of panic. It was late March, but where we were it was still very cold. On the day I heard the rumor I went and asked the German who was in charge of the laundry if it was true. He was an older man in his sixties. He was in the regular army, not the SS.

Most of the time he didn't bother with us but would constantly come and go from the laundry. The other girls stood behind me as I asked him if it was true that we were going to be evacuated. He got very agitated. He turned to me and said, "Be quiet. Where can they evacuate us to? From Berlin come the Russians, and from Hamburg come the British. We're surrounded. Where is there for us to go?"

He seemed so broken up by what he told me. I had to fight the urge to jump for joy at the news that we were surrounded. I didn't want him to see my happiness so I turned to the girls behind me and shouted at them in the same way he shouted at me, "Did you hear? It's terrible. We're surrounded. There's no place to evacuate us to."

Fortunately, he immediately walked out of the laundry because as soon as he did we all broke out in uncontrolled laughter.

We kissed and hugged and told everyone who came to the kitchen that we were soon to be liberated. But liberation was still a month and a half away.

We still had Appels in Neustadt. They used the numbers tattooed on our arms for the roll call. I remember standing on the Appel. This was on the 22nd of April. As we stood there an airplane flew very low over the camp. I could see the face of the pilot as he looked at us. Everyone said it was a British plane, and we were being photographed.

The next day was Hitler's birthday. As a present a large group of planes flew over the nearby airplane factory and destroyed it. The whole woods were set on fire. All around us were explosions. They went on for hours. But in all that time not even a splinter fell into our camp. That's how carefully they bombed the area. Even after the airplanes left there were still explosions as fuel and ammunition blew up.

I was in the laundry when the attack started. From the window the other girls and I watched the planes drop out of the sky. They flew in low and would release their bombs and then fly off again. From all around the camp the Germans fired anti-aircraft guns. A couple of times when we first saw a plane drop out of the sky we thought it was hit and was falling. All of us looking out of the window said at the same time, "Oh", very mournfully. Then when we saw the plane release its bombs and fly off we again in unison said, "Oh." But this time it was a very happy, "Oh."

All the work in the airplane factory stopped after the bombing. A few days later a group of our German guards came into the laundry. They each had civilian clothes in their hands that they wanted us to clean and press. While we were cleaning them the men would talk to us. They said how good they were to the Jews and to the other camp inmates. They talked about other Germans who were the mean ones, but they were all good.

They were also very afraid. You could hear the fear in their voices as they talked about the Russians. They talked about the great disaster that had befallen their country. Listening to them I wanted to grab one of them and shake him and say, "The great disaster that befell your country. You're the ones who started this. Don't you remember?" But I didn't.

When their clothes were ready they had us carefully fold them. Then they had us wrap them in paper so no one could see what they were carrying. With their packages under their arms they went to the door. They carefully peeked outside to make sure nobody was looking and left the laundry.

12
LIBERATION

The 1st of May started like so many other days. Around mid-day the girls and I were taking a break. We had just gotten a large piece of cheese from the kitchen, and I was cutting it up into equal parts for us to share. One of the girls who worked with us in the laundry, Cesha Koplowicz, walked in and said to me, "Mala, if I tell you some good news what would you give me?"

I said to her, "If it's really good news I'll give you my piece of cheese."

Cesha said, "The Germans have hung out a white flag."

I said, "That means they've surrendered, and the war is over."

We ran outside and looked around, but there was no white flag. We returned to the laundry. Cesha lost out on the piece of cheese, and I ate it.

An hour later we looked outside, and we saw a white flag hanging from the SS barracks. A few minutes later they took it back in. This went on all day. They didn't know what to do.

The camp commandant announced that he had gotten an order from Berlin to liquidate the camp and its inhabitants. But he said that he had no intention of hurting any of us or of destroying the camp. He was going to disregard the order.

The next morning we went to work as usual. As we were working a friend of mine named Noska Dadowich, she was from Paris, came into the laundry. She looked at us in amazement and asked, "You're still working? The Germans left during the night. There is nobody guarding the camp. Why are you working?"

We walked out of the laundry and looked at the gate and the guard towers. The sentries were gone. The guard towers were empty. The gate was locked, and the fence surrounding the camp was still electrified. So we were still trapped inside, but the SS were gone.

The moment we realized we were free our thoughts turned to food. Next to the laundry was a storage room. There the SS kept Red Cross packages that they hadn't distributed to the inmates. There was a locked door between the laundry and that storeroom. Above the door was a transom. We knew what was in that room and that there was food in those packages. Often we would talk about pushing Shindala through the transom to get at the packages. Shindala was the smallest among us.

Now that we had the chance, we rushed back into the laundry and forced open the transom. We lifted Shindala through the transom and lowered her to the floor of the storage room. She ran around the room and kept throwing the packages up to us through the transom.

A group of Russian women had the same idea. Just before Shindala could give us the last few packages they broke through a door on the other side of the storeroom. They looked around and saw that most of the packages were gone. They saw Shindala standing at the other door and our hands reaching for her through the transom. They started screaming and running at her. We got her back through the transom just before the Russian women got their hands on her.

They started banging on the door under the transom, threatening to break it down if we didn't give them the packages. I quickly filled a large pot of steaming hot water. I poked my head through the transom and threatened to pour the hot water on them if they didn't get away from the door. That scared them, and they left with the few packages that we didn't get.

Here we were, free. If we had thought about it we would not have had to fight over food. There would now be enough for everyone. But after years of thinking about nothing else but getting and hiding food that's the first thing we did.

Others did it too. After the war a cousin of mine told me about the time his camp was liberated. A friend of his, who was an Orthodox Jew, left the camp as soon as the Germans abandoned it. His friend ran into the nearby town. An hour later he came walking back into the camp dragging half a pig. My cousin asked him why he was dragging a pig now that they were liberated. His friend stopped, thought a second, shrugged his shoulders and dropped the pig. Without thinking he too couldn't pass up some extra food.

Near our camp was a French prisoner-of-war camp that had also been abandoned by the Germans. Some of the French came to our camp, broke open the gate, and shut off the electricity to the fence.

At first I was afraid to leave the camp. Some of the other women did, but I feared the Germans might turn around and come back. If they caught anyone outside the camp I was afraid they would kill them. So instead of leaving the camp I went to check out the SS barracks. Some of the other girls came with me, and we decided to move into a section of the SS barracks.

Later in the day a group of us got up the courage to go outside of the camp. As we walked out the gate my heart was pounding. I walked over to the edge of the road and lay down in the grass. It felt so good. I had almost forgotten what grass smelled like. What it felt like in my hands. What it felt like to just lie in it.

Lying there outside of the camp, thoughts of my family came to me. I hadn't thought about them for a while. Was my husband alive? My child? My parents, sisters and brothers? I didn't know. But I had seen how big the destruction was, and I feared that I was all that was left of all that I had known from before the war. I started to cry. I looked at the other girls, and some of them started crying too.

After awhile we got up and took a walk through the woods that surrounded the camp. It was spring, and it was a beautiful day.

We came to a road at the edge of the forest. It was the road that ran between Berlin and Hamburg. The road was full of fleeing Germans heading toward Hamburg. Full of people, some on horses, some in cars and on wagons, many just walking. All were weighed down with bedding, children and other belongings. A line of moving people that stretched endlessly in both directions.

A group of SS men were stopped in front of us. I recognized them by their uniforms. They were standing around a car parked by the side of the road. Some of the men were on horseback. They were talking among themselves trying to decide which way to go. They were unarmed and their uniforms were a mess.

We went over to them and I asked, "Where are you all running to?"

One of them answered back, "Don't you know? From Berlin come the Russians, and from Hamburg, the British. We're running to the British."

I said, "Why? So what if the Russians come?"

He looked at me and said, "Don't you know?"

Then he made a motion with his index finger across his throat.

I told the girls that we should return to the camp. I said if these people saw a smile on our faces they might do us harm. So we returned to the camp and to the SS barracks.

That same day near our camp, the British and the Russian armies met. Also on that day the first Russian soldiers entered our camp.

The very first Russian soldiers I saw were two officers. They were tall and very handsome. Later in the day more Russians came to the camp. Some of them tried to get friendly with the women inmates. The young soldiers started behaving badly. One of our girls was molested. Most of the time I stayed near the barracks to avoid them.

The first thing the Russians did was round up and imprisoned anyone who was a Kapo or Blockalteste in any of the camps. Not just here in Neustadt but in any of our former camps too. The Russian woman prisoners went around the camp with the soldiers pointing them out. They also encouraged the other inmates to point them out as well. All the ones who had important jobs in Auschwitz were pointed out to the Russians and arrested.

On the way back home to Poland, after we were liberated, we found this group of women that the Russians had arrested, in a prison camp. Some of them begged us to stop and tell the Russians that they weren't too bad to us. We just kept on going.

Another thing the Russians did when they first came into the camp was tell us that the inmates had 24 hours to take revenge on the Germans. I went with a group of women and a Russian soldier to a German's house outside of the camp. It was a poor house. The first one we came to in town. The rich ones were abandoned anyway.

We walked in and sitting by a table were two old people and a young child in a carriage. They were wearing pins that said that they were supporters of Rosa Luxenburg.

Rosa Luxenburg was the leader of the Communist party in Germany after the First World War. Luxenburg ran against Hitler in the election that brought the Nazi party to power.

The Russian soldier took out his gun and asked which one of us wanted it. The old couple began to cry and beg in German. They said they never wanted Hitler and that they never hurt anyone. None of us could take his gun.

I started to cry too and ran out of the house. I couldn't kill an old person or a child. I knew that the Germans had killed our old people and our children, but I could not do it. None of us women could. I don't know what would have happened if we had found other Germans other than old people or children. We all just returned to the camp.

Other groups of girls also went with soldiers to other houses. But they only found old people and children too. Nobody did any shooting that I knew of.

In the evening a tall Russian officer walked into our room in the SS barracks. One of our girls, her name was Sonia, spoke Russian. He told her that he hadn't slept in days and would just like to sleep for a few hours. He asked us to wake him before the morning. He slept so hard that a few times we tried to wake him, but we couldn't.

He slept for 24 hours. When we finally woke him and told him the time, he quickly got up and ran out of the room. Before he left he said he would be back in a few hours, and would we please prepare a meal for him.

When he returned he was drunk. He burst through the door. He stood in the doorway a moment. Then he drew his pistol and waved it at us. We all ran screaming and hid where we could. After a few seconds he put his gun down and said, "Come out, I won't hurt you."

Sonia asked him why he threatened us. He said that he'd been talking to some of the Russian inmates from the camp. They told him that the Jews were the ones who ran the gas chambers and crematoriums. That the Jews had killed his fellow Russians.

Sonia told him it was true. That Jews did work at the gas chambers and crematoriums, but the Germans forced them to work there. That both Jews and Russians were killed in the gas chambers. In the end the Jews who worked there were also killed in the same way.

He said he already knew that but wanted to hear it from us. He said he didn't hold us responsible.

I got very angry at all of this. To now be blamed for all that had happened was too much for me. I told the other girls that I was going home. I was not going to be a prisoner any longer.

Noska Dauvadobich lived in Paris before the war. She grew up in Boleslawiec and was a distance cousin of Alter's. We found each other in Auschwitz once, and again in Neustadt. She worked in the airplane factory before the bombing.

Noska now was organizing the group of French inmates. They were leaving the next day for home. She pleaded with me to go with her. France was free. It wasn't under the Russians. We had heard stories of what it was like in Poland. Everything was destroyed. There was no food. The Poles weren't welcoming returning Jews. There were new masters in Poland now, and we were seeing what they were like.

Noska suggested I stay in Paris until things got better in Poland before returning home, but I couldn't wait. Before I left home my father told me that when the war ended, no matter where I was, I was to return home. He told this to all of his children. I had to learn the fate of my family. Mostly I had to find my child.

Seven of us Jewish women got together, and made plans to leave the next day for Poland. Sonia had gotten to know a Russian officer. He wanted her to remain with him. She too wanted to find out what had happened to her family and told him she must go.

The next morning the seven of us were ready to set out for home. With me were Shindala, Rekinka, Sonia, Shasha, Esterka and Hanka. Esterka and Hanka were sisters.

We were ready to set out on foot. There was no other way to travel. The trains were not running yet. The group of French women was also ready to leave. The French army made a truck available to them. I went over and said good-bye to Noska. She asked me one more time to come with her. I said, "No," and we kissed each other good-bye. She handed me a note with an address and told me to write. For years after the war, we would send each other presents and greetings on the holidays.

As we were about to leave, Sonia's Russian officer came over to us leading a horse and wagon. He asked Sonia once again to say with him, but she said, "No." He said he was sorry she wouldn't stay, but he understood. He had gotten the wagon for us to make our trip easier. It was a four wheeled wagon pulled by one horse. We loaded it up with the few things we had and with some extra food. There was room in the wagon for all seven of us. We got in, and on the morning of the 4th of May we set out for home.

13
RETURNING HOME

We were part of a great flood of refugees moving every which way. Most of the people were going into Germany. We learned that the Russians and Poles were expelling great numbers of German civilians from Poland. We progressed very slowly. It was like moving against the tide.

The first day out of Neustadt we traveled along the road riding in our wagon. A group of young Russian soldiers came up along side of us. They were riding on bicycles. They started propositioning us, but we ignored them. Then one of them grabbed me and tried to pull me off the wagon. The other girls immediately grabbed me and held on. A few seconds later, the soldier gave up when he saw a car approach. I guess he was afraid it might have been someone important. Then he and the other soldiers rode away laughing.

Near the end of the day we were stopped by another group of Russian soldiers. They told us that they needed our horse and wagon and were going to confiscate them. We told them our story and how a Russian officer had given us the wagon. But they didn't listen. They gave us a few minutes to get our belongings. Then we continued our journey on foot.

When night fell we walked into a house by the side of the road. The house was empty. We found some potatoes and oil. We cooked some potato pancakes. In the middle of the night I got very sick. I had the runs all night. In the morning I could not travel. Sonya went out and found a Russian and got some rice from him. She made me eat the rice, and by the end of the day I felt a lot better. The next day I was well enough to travel, and we again set out for home.

Each night we stopped in a house along the road. Some were occupied, and some were not. The people in the occupied ones let us spend the night, and some fed us in the morning. At each house we got advice on which roads to take back to Poland. The most direct way was to go through Berlin, but people cautioned us against going that way since there was a lot of destruction. There was also a typhus epidemic in Berlin at the time because of the amount of unburied dead. At one house the owner prepared a map of side roads for us to follow so we could avoid Berlin.

Some houses we came into were full of people. There were many refugees on the road, and some houses by the road were packed with people seeking shelter for the night. In one house there were people sleeping all over the floor. It was that crowded. Among them were a group of Polish soldiers. We were afraid they would try to molest us during the night. We had blankets with us, so I told the girls to sleep two together wrapped in their blankets. I told them to wrap their arms around each other and hold each other tightly. Since we still had short hair, it would look like we were lovers sleeping together. This way it was less likely we would be disturbed. Many times that is how we got through the night safely.

The night was the scariest time. We always prayed to get through the night. In the empty houses we were afraid of someone coming in during the night. In the houses we shared with others we were afraid of them.

A few nights after we left Neustadt we were in a house with a group of other refugees. One of them had a radio. An announcement came over the radio that the war was over. The

Germans had surrendered. We were puzzled when we heard the news because we thought the war was already over by the time we were freed. We didn't realize that there was still fighting going on. There was a great deal of celebration going on that night on the road and in the houses. Strangers hugged and kissed. Drinks were passed around. Between the noise and the singing we didn't sleep at all that night.

The next day we ran into a group of Russian soldiers. They stopped to talk to us. They asked us where we were coming from and where we were going. At first we were cautious because they asked us if we were Jewish. When we found out that they too were Jewish, which I didn't believe until they started talking Yiddish, our happiness was overwhelming. We had not seen many Jews along the way, and to meet Jewish soldiers was very satisfying indeed.

They told us it was the Jewish holiday of Shavuos. We didn't know it was a holiday then. We had lost track of the dates of the Jewish holidays. The soldiers had some cheesecake, which was traditional on Shavuos, and they shared it with us. We spent the whole day, and most of the night, talking with them about the war. The next day they had to go where they were assigned, and we continued on our way home.

Along the way we learned that a hundred kilometers before Poznan a train was running to Poznan. Also, from Poznan another train was running all the way to Lodz. So we headed toward the train to Poznan.

After we boarded the train and we were on the way, a group of Polish soldiers came over to us. We were told that we were needed for a work group. They were rounding up people to help clear the rubble. We were told that the work was mandatory.

We refused to go with them. We told them we were just released from a labor camp and were going home. The soldiers grabbed us by the arms and pulled us out of our seats. Sonya ran into another car and saw a group of Russian officers standing nearby. She ran over to them and pleaded with them to help us. She told the Russians where we had come from and that the Poles now wanted to press us into a work gang. One of the officers came over and told the Poles to let us go. At first the Poles argued but backed down when the Russian threatened to get some of his friends from the other car.

I later found out that those Poles were AK, and the Russian knew that our lives would be in danger in the AK's hands. So once again we were liberated by the Russians.

We continued on the train for the rest of the journey to Poznan. After walking for 4 weeks across Germany, it was good to travel sitting down.

On the train I met a young Jewish man. As we approached Poznan he said to me that he had once run away from a camp nearby. He talked about his escape, which he did after another group of men was hung because they were caught escaping. Listening to him I had a feeling about my brother Wolf.

I asked him if he knew the men who were hung. He said he knew them all.

I said, "Was one of the men Wolf Liss?"

He said, "Yes, did you know him?"

I said, "He was my brother. Until now I thought he was still alive."

The train let us off on the outskirts of Poznan. We had to walk to the other side of the city to catch the train to Lodz. Poznan did not seem to have much damage or it had mostly been cleaned up by the time of our arrival. I only saw a few buildings that showed any damage.

My heart danced as we walked through the streets. Every street was full of German soldiers, now prisoners. Thousands and thousands of them were either sitting or were lined up in the streets and guarded by Russian soldiers. At every intersection we crossed we would look down the street in both directions. There was hardly a street that wasn't full of these Germans. They were waiting their turns to be loaded onto trains. In closed boxcars they were taken to Russia to be used as slave labor. Very few of them would survive to return to Germany.

At the end of the day we boarded a train to Lodz. The next morning we arrived in Lodz. In Lodz, the girls I traveled with made arrangements to go their separate ways home. We said our good-byes with tears and with promises to write to one another.

I went to my cousin's apartment hoping someone would be there. It was the same apartment I stayed in at the start of the war. I came up to her apartment and knocked on the door. The door was opened by my brother-in-law, Leipush. We were overcome with joy at seeing each other. Also in the apartment was my other brother-in-law, Itzhak Moshe. I learned from them that some other relatives and friends had also returned. Some had already gone on to Boleslawiec.

We spent the day talking about what had happened to us. My brothers-in-law had not heard anything about Alter. Nor had they heard about anyone else in my family. They wanted me to stay with them in Lodz, but I could not. I had to return home right away and see if anyone else came back. The next morning I took the train to my hometown.

I returned to Boleslawiec in the beginning of June, almost 3 years after I had gone into hiding. The town looked the same. There was no war damage except for the fire set by the Germans at the start of the war. It seemed like a lifetime ago.

I returned to the house that I grew up in to see the Mileskoys. When Mrs. Mileskoy saw me she cried and hugged me. We talked for a while. I learned that a few of the others who had returned were all staying together at the same house in the town.

The house had belonged to a widow named Kohn. We used to call her the Gailtis Kohn because her husband had had a yellow beard. Gail means yellow in Yiddish. Her four sons had survived the war. She had not. They were all there. Also there was my friend from Auschwitz, Rose Etta; two of my cousins, Yanta and Jizka Krzepizka, who I had seen briefly in Auschwitz; and a young man from our town named Kupple Miller. I went to see them, and they invited me to stay there too.

I went to the apartment we had lived in before I went into hiding, and my parents were taken away. The Polish woman who lived there let me in and told me that nothing of mine was still there. But I saw things that were, like the bed spreads and curtains. I mentioned them, and she said that they were the only things of mine, and I could take them if I wanted. I saw other things, but they weren't worth the trouble, so I just said, "No," and left.

Outside the building a Pole, who I knew to be a good man, came over to me. He greeted me and told me to come to his apartment. He had a number of my things. He told me how the Germans auctioned off the Jewish belongings after the Jews were taken from the town. He had some furniture from my apartment. He also had some pictures that he found in the furniture that he had saved. The pictures he gave me, but the furniture he offered to sell back to me for the amount he paid. I didn't have any money or any place to put the furniture, so I told him that I could not buy them back, but I thanked him for the pictures. They were more precious to me than the furniture.

I found other Poles with other items from my family. Small items some gave back to me. One Pole I went to see had my father's sewing machines. He was the town's tailor. When I came to his house he frightened me so much I thought he was going to kill me. He asked me if I planned to stay in the town. There was so much hatred in his eyes I right away said, "No." I guess he was afraid I would demand he return the machines, and he would have to give them to me. I left as quickly as I could. I felt lucky he let me leave his house alive. I stopped looking for anything else.

I returned on a Thursday, and on the following Monday or Tuesday my sister Fay came home. She had first come to Czestochowa. There she met a young man from our town who told her of my return. I did not know that she was alive until I saw her.

As soon as she came home she wanted me to go with her to Lodz, to meet the man she wanted to marry. His name was Simon Susskind. They had met in the Lager Fay had worked in. He had gone to his hometown to learn the fate of his family. They had arranged to meet in Lodz in a few days.

We returned to Lodz, to the apartment of my brother-in-law Leipush. There I met my future brother-in-law, Simon.

Simon's father had been a big industrialist in their hometown of Bielitz. They owned a factory for weaving wool cloth. When the Germans first came into the town they took a number of its leading citizens as hostages. Simon was one of them.

He had spent the war as a prisoner of the Germans. He was part of the early labor brigades that built some of the concentration and work camps, first in Poland and later in Germany. He was part of the labor that built Auschwitz.

Simon couldn't stay in Poland. In Bielitz the Russians were arresting the families of the wealthier citizens. The Russians were looking for him. He had been warned just in time and left the city. He was afraid that if he stayed in Poland they would find him and arrest him.

For many returning Polish Jews there were problems. Many of us were talking about leaving. We weren't welcome back, and it was beginning to feel unsafe for us.

Fay and Simon decided to go to Czechoslovakia. Simon had been married before the war. His wife died early in the war in one of the camps. Her family was from Moravska Ostrava, a city in Czechoslovakia just across the Polish border. They were going to see if anybody from his wife's family had returned.

The western part of Czechoslovakia was under American administration at the time. Since Simon's wife was Czech he knew he could get a Czech identification card for himself. Once they got married, Fay would also have Czech papers. They planned to arrange papers for me too. Fay was going to return for me when they had those papers.

The next day Fay and Simon left for Czechoslovakia.

Nobody else from my family had returned home. I decided to travel to Warsaw and learn the fate of my daughter.

I had heard that in Warsaw there was a Jewish agency that was helping people find other members of their families.

In every city, where there was a Jewish community, there was a Jewish agency. Every Jewish agency had lists. There were lists of survivors, lists of transports, lists of where the inmates from one camp went when the camps were moved. There was information on who returned home, and messages for those who still might come home.

People just traveled from city to city looking at lists and bringing one list from one place to another. Any word about a member of one's family, or even a word about someone who might have known something about them, would send people off looking for that person or that list.

Once on a train I met a group of young men with a list of survivors from the camp they had been in. On their list I saw the name of Lunik Yakobovich. These men knew Lunik and that he had come from Boleslawiec. They told me that Lunik was now in Germany. I told them that Lunik's sister, Estarka, was alive and living with the Polish family that hid her during the war. She was not far from where we were. I told them that Estarka thought Lunik dead. One of the young men left the train and traveled to where Estarka was. He brought her the news about her brother and made arrangements for her to go to him in Germany.

Though there was some happy stories like Estarka's and Lunik's most of the searching was in vain or ended in sadness.

Itzhak Moshe came with me to Warsaw. When we got there we made our way to the Jewish agency in Praga. Praga was across the river from Warsaw. Warsaw was greatly damaged by the war. The ghetto was all rubble, not a building standing.

The Jewish agency building was full of people milling about inside and out. As soon as I walked in I saw Alla

Dirchwald. We were thrilled to find each other alive. We sat and told each other what had happened to us since we had last seen each other. She was also there looking for information about her family.

After waiting a few hours I met with a man who was to help me find my daughter. He took down the information about the dates when she was taken out of Warsaw. He went and looked through lists that the Russians had confiscated from the Germans. The Germans were very thorough and listed everything. The lists he looked through gave the dates and the destination of all the trains that took the Jews out of the ghetto.

The trains that left Warsaw on the dates of the Aktion in January 1943 all went to Treblinka. He sadly told me that I didn't need to look any further. The records showed that almost all the people from those trains went directly into the gas chambers, especially the children.

I can't say I was surprised at the news, but still I had hoped for a miracle. And that hope had kept me going many times. I broke down and cried. Alla stayed with me till I was better.

Itzhak Moshe and I spent the rest of the day at the agency. We looked through records hoping to find information about any other members of our families, but we found nothing. In the evening we took a train back to Lodz. The next day I returned to Boleslawiec.

A few days after I returned from Warsaw, Fay returned from Czechoslovakia with papers for me. Together we left Poland for the last time. I had intended to return with papers for my two cousins, but I didn't make it in time.

It took me a few weeks after I got to Czechoslovakia to get papers for my cousins. By then the Polish-Czech border had been sealed. With our Czech papers it would be no problem returning to Czechoslovakia. The problem was getting into Poland. I had no identification that said I was a Pole.

The mail wasn't working very well yet. It was too undependable. With the danger to the Jews in Poland getting worse, I had to get my cousins out as fast as I could. Also I wanted to leave word with someone in case my husband returned. I had to tell someone where I was so that he could find me. I knew that a lot of survivors were still in hospitals. Every day I would hear of another who had returned home. I prayed that the next one would be Alter.

Rose Etta and my two cousins tried to leave Poland and come to where I was in Czechoslovakia. They were arrested at the border by the Polish guards and spent a few days in jail. When they were released they were sent back to Boleslawiec. Without proper papers they could not get out of Poland.

We were staying in Moravska Ostrava, which was along the Polish border. I found out that a group of workers came every day from Poland to work in Moravska Ostrava. Each evening, in a group, they would return to Poland. I found out where the workers crossed the border. I waited along the road leading to the border crossing. As the group of workers came down the road I stepped in line with them and walked up to the check point.

A young border guard was checking everybody's papers. When he got to me I handed him my Czech papers. He asked me where I was going. I told him that in the town where these men came from lived a man who had been in a concentration camp with my husband. My husband hadn't returned, and I was going to find out what this man knew about him.

The guard gave me back my papers and told me that I could not go across. He said that I was Jewish and that it would be too dangerous for me in Poland. I pleaded with him to let me go. He just kept saying, "No."

I wouldn't leave him alone. I started crying. Finally, he took his rifle off of his shoulder and pointed it at me. He screamed at me, "God in heaven. Don't you understand? The Poles will kill you. Go back. I will never let you pass."

I had no choice. I returned to where Fay and Simon were staying.

Weeks later while traveling on a train from Frankfurt to Wesbaden in Germany, I read of an attack on Jews in Boleslawiec. The date of the attack was the day after I tried to cross into Poland.

The story told of an attack by a group of Poles on a house that Jews were staying in. It was the Kohn's house. There they killed all of its inhabitants. The Poles that did the killing were members of the AK. The story listed the names of the 8 people killed. They were three of the Kohn brothers, Mosha Rusick, Maier Markowitz, Rose Etta and my two cousins.

Maier Markowitz had survived the war hiding out in Czestochowa with his wife and child. His family was still in Czestochowa as he returned to Boleslawiec to collect some of their possessions. He was staying at the Kohn's house the day of the attack.

A week earlier two of the widow Kohn's sons had gone to Germany to find a place for the family to stay. One of them had returned home the day before the attack with travel papers for his other two brothers. They were in middle of packing to leave as the AK arrived.

Had I gotten across the border the day I tried to cross, I, too, would have been in that house when the AK came.

Months later, in Germany, I met Kupple Miller. He gave me 4 photos that the Russians had taken of the murdered Jews.

The day before the killings Kupple, who had also been staying at the Kohn's house, went to a nearby village to collect some money that was owed to his family. He spent the night in the village and returned to Boleslawiec in the morning. He arrived shortly after the attack took place. Promised protection by the Russians, he remained to identify and bury the dead. As soon as that was done he left Poland for good.

We didn't remain long in Moravska Ostrava. Fay and Simon got married, and then we moved on to Prague.

Prague was a beautiful city. I spent a lot of time walking around. The city was full of statues and museums. The High Holy days came and we went to synagogue. I started living again.

The government and other organizations helped camp survivors. One organization arranged us go to Marrainbad, a world famous health resort, for 4 weeks.

The Allies agreed among themselves that Russia alone would occupy Czechoslovakia. Until then, the Americans administered the western part with the Russians administering the east.

Simon had some acquaintances in the newly formed Czech army. They advised him to leave with the Americans. They knew that the government under the Russians would be Communist. With Simon's background he would have a problem. Simon's first wife had a cousin living in America. With some family in America Simon would be able to apply for immigration.

We left Czechoslovakia in November as the Americans were pulling out. We were going to the American zone in Germany. Fay was pregnant so she stayed in the apartment in Prague while Simon and I went to Germany. After we got a place there, Simon would return for Fay. Also, Fay stayed in

Prague in case we could not get across the border, we would still have a place to return to.

At the border checkpoint a Czech officer looked through our suitcases and our papers. He said the papers were not proper, and by right we should not be allowed to leave. He guessed why we were leaving and said he would help us. He got a soldier and told him to lead us across the border so we could avoid the guards and the checkpoint on the German side. The soldier led us through some woods for about an hour, until we could see a town. He pointed the town out to us and said it was called Tirschenreuth. It was in Germany. The soldier turned around and went back to Czechoslovakia.

As soon as Simon and I entered the town we stopped to rest. I saw a woman walking toward us. When she got close I recognized her as Figua Prince from my hometown. I called her name, and she looked at me for a moment wondering who I was. Then she recognized me and came running, calling my name out loud. We hugged and kissed.

Figua Prince took us to her apartment where we stayed the night talking about what had happened to each of us. She told me that Estarka Yackabovich was nearby in a city called Hof. The next day we went to Estarka's.

I stayed at Estarka's, in Hof, while Simon went back for Fay. It took them two weeks to get themselves smuggled across the border.

Before we left Prague we made friends with an American officer who was Jewish. When we told him we were leaving for Germany, he told us he was being transferred to Frankfurt. He offered to have some of our things transported to Germany for us. We left six suitcases with him.

From Hof we went to Frankfurt to get our things. Then we moved to Wiesbaden. Simon's mother was from Manhime, near Wiesbaden. Simon had been there many times before the war and knew the area very well. So we settled there.

In Wiesbaden, the Jewish Agency set up an organization. They settled displaced people who were coming into the American zone. They helped people search for members of their families, and reunited them when they could. They also helped people learn the fate of those who did not return.

The Jewish organization got us proper papers, some money, and gave us an address where we could live.

The address was Richistraser 3. It was the home of a former Nazi. The house was damaged during the war by Allied bombing. All the other homes on the street were taken over by the Americans, but not this one. Because of the bomb damage the Americans would not live there.

When we got to the house, the owner would not let us in. We had to threaten him before he gave in. He lived there with his wife and daughter. We divided up the house so we would not have to see each other.

A short while later my brother-in-law, Itzhak Moshe, came to live with us. Leipush was still in the Polish army and would not leave Poland for two more years. I did not see Leipush again until we were in America.

Itzhak Moshe continued to look for Alter. Some information took him to Salzhime, a city near Frankfurt. There he found a man who was with Alter. He had held Alter in his arms as Alter died just 3 weeks before their liberation.

Through the Jewish organization I also learned what had happened to my parents, my sister Eudel, and most of the Jews from my hometown. The fate of my oldest brother Gavriel, I did not learn until 1978. What had happened to his wife and child I still do not know.

In 1978 I took my first trip to Israel. A cousin of mine, who was living in Israel, had met a man who had been in a camp with Gavriel. From him I learned of my brother's death.

Late in 1942, around the time I was trying to get to my brother from Czestochowa, Gavriel, and the man who told the story, escaped from a labor camp. The Germans learned of their escape, and chased them through the forest. The Germans caught up with them at a river. The two men jumped into the river and started swimming across. The Germans stopped at the riverbank, and opened fire. Halfway across the river my brother screamed, and stopped swimming. He did not make it across. The other man did. When he got to the other side he looked back for a second, before he continued running. He saw my brother's body being swept down the river.

14
AMERICA

We made friends with a lot of the Americans living on our street. From one of then I took English lessons. I also worked for him as an interpreter. We traveled around buying antique furniture from the Germans. He paid very little for the furniture, as the Germans needed the money. The antiques he sent to America, and he paid me for helping him.

One thing the Americans had a lot of and the Germans had very little of was cigarettes. With our connections with the Americans we were able to get a lot of cigarettes. They practically gave them to us. We would trade the cigarettes to the Germans for money and other valuables, which we in turn would sell to the Americans. We made enough money that Simon and I were able to buy a house. The houses were cheap at the time because of the poverty of the Germans.

1946 brought a number of marriages and some children in our community of survivors. Fay and Simon had their first child, a boy, born on the 24th of April.

At Channuka, in December, I went with Fay and Simon to the synagogue for a party. It was so crowded by the time we got there that there was no place for us to sit. We stood in the back of the synagogue. Standing next to us were two men and a woman. One of the men and Simon went outside and brought back some crates and boards and made a bench and table out of them. We all sat down and got to know each other.

The man who went outside with Simon was Maier Brandsdorfer. The other man was his brother, Joseph. The woman was Joseph's wife, Paula. They were all from Chrzanow, near Krakow, in southern Poland. At the start of the war they were able to escape to Russia. The Russians sent them to labor in Siberia during the war. When the war ended they came to the American zone rather than return home because of the troubles the Jews were having in Poland, and because they did not want to stay under the Russians any longer.

In February, Maier and I were engaged to be married. Itzhak Moshe got engaged at this time too. Fay, Simon and their young son left for America. In March, during Purim, I got married. An American chaplain performed the ceremony. By May the next year, our first child was born. We named him after his two grandfathers, Mordechai Joshua.

After Fay and Simon were settled in America they made arrangements for us to come over.

Our trip to America started with a stay in a camp in Frankfurt for a few weeks. Then a stay in a camp in Breman for another few weeks. Then in another camp, in Hamburg. In each camp we waited until our name was called to move to the next place closer to the ship and to America.

We boarded the ship, named the Marina Flecher, the last week of March 1949. The ship was an American troop transport. There were 1100 passengers. The men and women were separated into large dormitories during the trip. Maier got into some trouble with the ship's American officers because he kept sneaking in to see the baby and me. During the trip I was seasick the whole time, so they finally let Maier come and spend some time with us and help me out.

Twelve days after leaving Hamburg we landed in Boston. It was April 5, 1949. The mayor of Boston greeted the ship. There was also a large crowd and a marching band. The mayor made a speech that left everyone crying. He spoke about us, the people on the boat: how we were all immigrants and displaced persons: about our struggle and what we had survived. I don't remember much of the mayor's speech, but I remember the marching band. It was the first time I had seen a band led by girls twirling sticks. I was very impressed by this my first sight of America.

The Joint Committee gave everyone on the ship 10 dollars so we would have some money in our pockets until we got settled. Family or friends met some of the people at the ship. Others had arrangements made for them to travel to their destinations. Simon had made all of the arrangements for us, and we took the train to New York. Fay, Simon and their son met us at the train station when we arrived in New York.

Fay and Simon were living in Brooklyn, and we settled there too. Many in our neighborhood were Jews newly arrived from Europe, with shared experiences and starting new lives in a new land.

The map highlights many of the locations mentioned in this book. The Death March of January 1945, is the approximate route my mother took. Gross Rosen was just one of several destinations for death marchs from Auschwitz in January 1945. All of then going west away from the advancing Russians. Many of the other marches were nearly twice as long as the one to Gross Rosen.

WARSAW
GHETTO

—— GHETTO WALL

AREA STILL LEGALLY INHABITED -
FALL 1942 TO SPRING 1943

By the time my mother arrived in Warsaw, most of the Jewish
residents had been forcefully removed. The ghetto once held
over 400,000 people. By the fall of 1942 the population had
been reduced to around 60,000. Only essential workers and
their families were allowed to remain. There were a number of
undocumented people hiding in getto, including members of
the Jewish Fighting Organization. The ghetto was destroyed
by May 1943 after the Passover uprising.

Machel Liss, Mordechai Liss' father. A fruit grower
from Wielun, Machel Liss died in 1928 at the age of 97.

Esther Pearl Schenk, Blima Liss' mother.

Mordechai Liss, (on left) with two of his friends. Photo taken 1905, in central Russia, at their army post. Aaron Pawlowitz (in the center) later married Pesa Liss, Mordechai's sister.

Mala Liss, and her brothers, Wolf and Gavriel.
Photo taken, 1928, by the town's photographer.
Gavriel was then serving in the Polish Army.

Photo taken by the town's photographer in 1928. Just for fun Mala Liss (on right) and her friend, Manya Altman, dressed up in their brothers' army uniforms for this photo. Both of their brothers were home on leave. The photographer liked this photo so much that he put it in his shop window, which was on the town's main street. When Mala's father saw the photo he got very angry at her, feeling that it was improper behavior for a young woman to dress up in a man's clothes.

Wolf Liss, (standing left) and his brother Gavriel. Seated (on left) is their sister Mala, and their cousin Rachael Liss, 1935.

Left to right, Eudel, Mala and Fay Liss.
Photo taken by the town's photographer, 1937.

Mala (standing) and Eudel Goldrat, Alter's older sister.
Photo taken by the town's photographer, 1932.

Eudel Liss, 1937, in her Zionist Youth uniform.

Wolf Liss, 1937, while in the Polish army.

Gavriel Liss, and Hinda Ruthy,
right before they were married in 1937.

Pearl Liss, 5 months old. Gavriel and Hinda Ruthy's daughter.

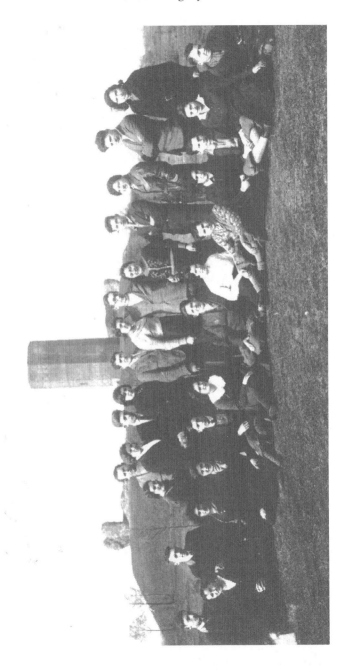

The Zionist Youth Organization of Boleslawiec, 1937. Photo taken along the river Prosna. The ruins of King Boleslaw's castle are in the background. Mala Liss is standing in the center wearing a dark skirt and light sweater. Standing to her left is their teacher, Chiam Landau, who traveled to all the small towns in the region organizing young Jews and teaching then Hebrew and Zionist songs. Chiam left for Palestine before the war started, and later became a government minister in Israel.

Pictured, 1st row: Kupple Miller, Brandel Kohn, Kupple Prince, Zisel Krzepizka, Eudal Liss, Wolf Liss, Zisel Russek, Yankel Kohn, Hanna Prince, Motel Russek, Yanta Krzepizka, Hershel Russek, Fay Liss, Mosha Russek

2nd row: Hanka Russek, Abush Pinkus, Toba Froman, Itzhak Moshe Goldrat, Yanta Rachel Goldrat, Anlibe Altman, Mala Liss, Chiam Landau, Leah Russek, Sholma Kohn, Krindel Kohn, Gavriel Liss, Shalmis Istik

Nunyala Goldrat, 16 months old. Photo taken November, 1939, a few months after the start of the war.

Alter Goldrat, Photo taken before the war.

Yanta and Jizka Krzepizka, 1938. Mala Liss' first cousins. Yanta (top) was born in 1917 and Jizka in 1925. Yanta and Jizka lived through the war only to be killed on their return home by the Polish Home Army. From a family of 7 girls and 2 boys only one brother survived. He had left for Argentina before the war started.

Yanta Liss (seated) and her sister Sara (standing on the left.) Next to Sara is a friend of theirs. This photo was taken in May 1942, in the labor camp of Inowroclaw. It was sent home with some letters in the summer, 1942.

The following 4 photographes, taken in Boleslawiec, by the Russians, in October 1945, only hours after the early morning attack by the AK on the Kohn's house. The Jews who had returned to Boleslawiec were staying in this house. All the Jews staying in the house that day were killed. They were the 3 Kohn brothers, Yanta and Jizka Krzepizka, Mosha Russek, and Rose Etta Pinkus. Also killed was Maier Markowitz. Maier survived the war hiding out in Czestochowa with his wife and child. He left them in Czestochowa during this trip to Boleslawiec to collect some of his family's possessions.

The photos were given to Kupple Miller. The day before the killings Kupple, who had also been staying at the Kohn's house, went to a nearby village to collect some money that was owed to his family. He spent the night in the village and returned to Boleslawiec in the morning. He arrived shortly after the attack took place. Promised protection by the Russians, he remained to identify and bury the dead. As soon as that was done he left Poland for good.

Mendel Kohn

Maier Markowitz, Mosha Russek and Shia Hersh Kohn

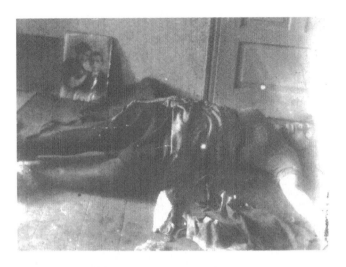

Yanta Krzepizka

Rose Etta Pinkus, Jizka Krzepizka and Yankel Kohn

This document was provided by the United States Holocaust Memorial Museum. The Russian government gave the museum copies of their microfilm collection of Auschwitz documents that the Russians removed from Auschwitz after it's liberation. This is the form my mother signed when she was tattooed after her arrival. The number at the top of the form is the number tattooed on her arm. Her signature is at the bottom.

Fay and Simon Susskind's wedding photo.
Czechoslovakia, 1945.

Maier and Mala Brandsdorfer's wedding photo.